M000023103

INDIVISIBLE

Stroud & Hall Publishers
P.O. Box 27210
Macon, Ga 31221
www.stroudhall.com

©2005 Martha Zoller

All rights reserved.
Printed in the United States of America
First Edition

The paper used in this publication meets the minimum requirements
of American National Standard for Information Sciences—
Permanence of Paper for Printed Library Materials.
ANSI Z39.48–1984. (alk. paper)

Library of Congress Cataloging-in-Publication Data

Zoller, Martha, 1959-
Indivisible : uniting values for a divided America / by Martha Zoller.
p. cm.
ISBN 0-9745376-4-0 (hardcover : alk. paper)
1. United States--Social conditions--1980
2. Social values--United States.
3. United States--Politics and government.
I. Title.

HN59.2.Z65 2005
320.6'0973--dc22

2005023112

To Cathy,
Happy Birthday
Godspeed,
Martha Zoller

INDIVISIBLE

Uniting Values for a Divided America

Martha Zoller

Dedication

Patti Benton Stephenson
1953-2004

Table of Contents

The American Pendulum

Foreword

BY ZELL MILLER

A fellow Georgian and writer, Flannery O'Connor, once wrote, "you shall know the truth and the truth shall make you odd." I can't think of a better way to introduce to you both Martha Zoller and her book, *Indivisible*. Martha has made finding the truth her life's pursuit, and, as you will read later in this book, it has made her stand out and even seem odd by some standards. She must have seemed odd to the ultra-feminists for pursuing and developing her own career while raising fine children and being there for them. She must have seemed odd to the leaders of her former party of Democrats because she recognized early in the '80s the party's drift away from grassroots concerns. She must have seemed odd to the Michael Dukakis campaign when even though she supported him she had the wisdom to speak truth to power, telling him he seemed cold and aloof to Southern voters and couldn't win votes that way. She probably even seems odd today to those who view America as an evenly divided checkerboard of red and blue states.

In *Indivisible*, Martha Zoller helps us find the way to the white light of the truth about America, leading us out of the red/blue morass that currently plagues our political landscape. Her book and her work are based on the conviction that truth isn't owned by any party and America is a great land because the majority of her citizens long for that truth. The liberal media machine that makes a sport of covering general elections is getting traction for the myth that we are a divided nation. They would have you think that America is split down the middle, when the reality yields a much different picture. When the red/blue map is broken down by city/region, it is clear that traditional conservative American values blanket this great land, while the more populous cities who serve as home of the media elite propagate the divisive and irresponsible liberal agenda. I crisscrossed this land of ours while campaigning for President Bush in 2004. I didn't see the divided America that the media elites drone on and on about. I saw the America Martha Zoller describes. It's an America that knows how to do the right things for the right reasons and nothing less, Democrat or Republican. It's an America that can judge whether a candidate is in love with this country and willing to fight for her or simply in love with being in office.

Martha's love of this country is obviously manifest. As a fellow history buff, she takes seriously the important moments in our nation's history. She holds as sacred the founding fathers and their intent for what America was to be. Her fidelity to the America Thomas Jefferson envisioned prevents her from following the rest of the herd in reading into the Constitution what's clearly not there. In *Indivisible*, Martha offers a lesson in civics that benefits the welcomed legal immigrant as well as the seasoned politician. She lovingly writes of our country, how its government is organized, and the values on which it stands. She is informed, yes, but she is smitten as well.

Martha's *Indivisible* is the natural outcome of a woman who proudly confesses her dependence on God. As a fellow believer, she recognizes that foundation of the vision of our American forefathers. The Creator blessed us with her for such a time as this. If we are wise, we will read *Indivisible* with the hope that truth will make us odd as well.

Zell Miller
August 2005

Acknowledgments

First I want to thank God for being merciful to me and blessing me so richly in my life. I would be nowhere without a deep and abiding faith in God. One of those blessings is a family who loves me. I have a husband, Lin, who just gets better as he gets older and who tries to do the things I want him to do. I used to think I was the easy one to live with and I have learned with age and the onset of menopause that I am not. Also, my wonderful children, who keep me honest when they remind me, "Mom, does it have to be *The Martha Zoller Show* around here all the time?" I am learning every day from them and they are turning out to be pretty great people. Chip, Mark, Ricky, and Suzanne are the cornerstones that I make my schedule around and they keep my feet on the ground.

I also want to thank Sen. Zell Miller for being a good friend and a cheerleader of mine, and I am humbled at the friendship that has been given to me by Sean Hannity. He is a nice as he seems on the radio and at a time when he is on a shooting star, he has always found time to be a friend in this business and to give good advice. I also could not have done the sections that referenced the Declaration of Independence without the help of Hank Sullivan, the author of *In a Larger Sense.* Hank was invaluable to this project.

Herb Blondheim was my longtime boss at Rich's in Atlanta when I was a buyer there and he gave me the best advice of my life. I was a go-getter assistant buyer and I knew that I could be better than anyone at the next level. He took me to lunch and told me to concentrate on doing well the job that I was in, rather than always looking to the next one, or I would never get to the next one. He also taught me something about balance. He said put your family first or one day you will come home early and your children will ask you, "What are you doing here?"

My parents, Frank and Juanita Mitchell, provided the discussion at the dinner table. I wish my father could have seen my success, but I had a listener tell me once that she felt like she knew my dad because of the way I talked about him. That was the greatest compliment she could have given me. My father taught me about duty, honor and country, and my mother taught me about the value of faith and hard work. I will be forever indebted to them both. My sisters, Pam Gunter and Linda Tuminella, gave me just enough of a hard time to keep me straight and my brother, Frank A. R. Mitchell, taught me how to stand my ground in a debate.

To the Jacobs family and the WDUN family, the opportunities that I have had to grow *The Martha Zoller Show* franchise from Gainesville, Georgia, cannot be measured. From Amy Harrison picking my son up from the orthodontist to Jay Jacobs, our owner, who early in my career colored with my daughter on his conference room table while I finished my program, there isn't a better company to work for in radio. Jacobs Media understands the relationship between work and family. Ember Bishop is the newest member of the team and will help move the franchise to the next level.

My church family at Gainesville First United Methodist Church and all the activities and worship opportunities that it provides and all the prayer that goes out from that place provides a support in everything I do as well as a safe haven for children and families in an unstable world.

To Cecil Staton and all of the supportive and kind folks at Stroud and Hall Publishing, who believed I had this book in me, who managed the process and served as a sounding board, I thank you.

Thanks to all of the bookers, publicists, authors, celebrities and politicians with whom I have worked with over the years. You are the fabric of America and this big city girl turned small town woman is better for having worked with all of you.

To my two best friends in the world, Karin Pendley Koser and Juanita Clavijo Hulsey. They have been with me in all the firsts in my life and I love them.

Finally, I dedicate this book to Patti Benton Stephenson, my dear friend that we all lost to breast cancer in 2004. She was a light in the world. Patti and I went through teenagers together and she remained a positive, strong and steadfast friend for as long as I can remember. When I learned Patti was sick, I couldn't imagine life without her. God had a different plan for her and she inspired me to live life to the fullest. She had a laugh that could make the worst day better and when I think of her—as I often do—I can't help but smile.

Introduction

In the aftermath of the 2004 election, many pundits argued that America is a politically divided nation. The raw numbers certainly seem to back up this notion. However, when we look at the electoral map—the one with the red and blue, divided by state, region, county, or city—drastic political division is almost impossible for us believe. The electoral map reminds us of what Ed Gillespie, Republican National Committee Chairman in 2004, said to me in the early days of the campaign and what I repeated many times on radio, television, and in print: "the red states are getting redder and the blue states are getting purple."

When all the votes were counted, the locations of the largest concentrations of Democratic votes was striking. The Left in this country is stacked in the cities, where the liberal media moguls and the big govenment bureaucrats live, work, and play. Apart from these areas of Democratic concentration, what remains are wide-open spaces of red, encompassing the vast geographical expanse that is America.

Most people believe there is more common ground than division in the attitudes of Americans across this vast expanse. News programs and newspaper articles, however, often include both sides of an issue, leading us to assume there are just as many people on one side of an issue as on another. But that representation of an equal and opposite point of view doesn't make sense to those of us getting up every day and building our lives in America. Certainly we have disagreements on issues, even within the red states, but the range of views on issues is much narrower nationwide than the overwhelmingly liberal, controversy-loving media would have us believe. In the end, America is a center-right country—historically, ideologically, and practically.

Most politicians have to go through a primary process in which they must appeal to their core constituency. When campaigning among themselves for votes, Democrats go to the left on issues and Republicans go to the right on issues. In the general election, however, politicians must return to the center to pick up the all-important undecided voter. In the 2004 presidential election, the distance John Kerry had to travel to get to that coveted middle was much farther than the distance George Bush had to go. Any baseball outfielder can tell you the distance to center-right is shorter from right field than it is from left field. The same is true in national presidential elections. It's what Karl Rove, the architect for the campaign to reelect the president, and Ken Mehlman, the president's campaign manager and current chairman of the Republican National Convention, were banking on in the 2004 presidential election. They understood what the political pundits refuse to believe—that most Americans hold political views right-of-center.

Over time I began to think of this political reality as the "elephant in the room." Traditionally, this phrase is used to describe something everyone knows to be real but refuses to acknowledge. For me, particularly in our current political climate, the "elephant in the room" is the conservative makeup of the American majority and the obvious solutions to the issues that are important to this majority. It is time the huge elephant in our nation is recognized.

Finding My Way

I have always tried to make an impact. Without hard work, seized opportunity, and faith in God, I would not have been seen or heard of outside of my own community. The concept of what is right and what is wrong has driven me professionally and personally though many sleepless nights. People have always looked at me as a person who leads and with that influence has come great responsibility. Some of it I have handled well, and some of it I wish I could go back and do again.

Some of my first memories are of defending my positions at the dinner table. My siblings are six to twelve years older than I, so in many ways growing up I was an only child. Like many only children, I have always had a need to be heard. But I also wanted to say something my older teenaged siblings would think was smart. So I read. I would read *Life* magazine every week just to have something worthwhile to say. My brother, in particular, was the great debater while my sisters were the touchy-feely type. I just knew he was always right, and if I could go toe-to-toe with him, I had accomplished something.

My father would push me to talk to anyone who walked by. "Put your hand out and tell them who you are," he would say. So I did. Whenever I had a question neither my father nor mother could answer, he would say, "Write a letter to the president." So I would. I wrote letters to all kinds of people and kept the replies in a blue suitcase that my sister, Pam, gave me. I still write letters, and I encourage others to do the same. In this world of immediacy, we have to hold on to the respect we show when we take time to sit down to write, address, and mail a letter.

Throughout high school, college, and into my early twenties, I bought into the liberal line. I thought Republicans were against minorities and that they didn't want equality for women. I thought abortion was wrong, but that a woman had the right to choose. I thought Ronald Reagan was the problem with America. It is my shame now that I didn't appreciate until he left office what President Reagan did for this country. At the time, I knew he had made me feel better about being an American, but I didn't appreciate the scope of what he accomplished.

Sometime in 1986, I was flipping through the television channels and saw Newt Gingrich deliver a speech on C-Span. I had just moved into his district in Georgia, but I believed all the negative sound bites about him, so I wasn't going to watch. *What can this male chauvinist pig teach me?* I thought. But for some reason, I paused to watch. At the end of the speech, I thought, *Am I wrong about Newt Gingrich? This guy makes a lot of sense.* Once I started reading about him, I found that, like me, he is a history buff. Once I moved to reading some of his articles and speeches, I realized I had been wrong about his ideology. Soon it occurred to me that if I had been wrong about him, what else had I been wrong about?

I didn't want to do anything rash; it would have been pretty radical for me to come out of the liberal closet as a Newt Gingrich Republican. So I began doing my homework. I knew the Democratic National Convention was going to be in Atlanta, so I began reading up on the candidates. Michael Dukakis was getting some good press, and he seemed to be a blend of conservative fiscal policy with liberal social policy, which is where I thought I was. Dukakis also had an office in Atlanta, so I began to volunteer there in late 1986. Throughout the campaign and the election, I had wonderful experiences. I had an American-made car, so I was able to be a driver for Kitty Dukakis, Olympia Dukakis, Sam Donaldson and many high-level campaign staffers. I even got to share a meal or two with Governor Dukakis in Atlanta.

Once when I was driving Mrs. Dukakis, she asked me why I was supporting her husband. I said I had some concerns that the Democratic Party was leaving me. I was concerned they didn't have a place for a working person who was upwardly mobile, fiscally conservative, and socially moderate. I thought Governor Dukakis met those goals. Then she said, "You ought to be in one of our commercials. You have to meet Michael." When we arrived at the airport, the governor was having lunch. Mrs. Dukakis said, "Michael, you need to talk to this girl." He asked me why his message wasn't getting out in the South. I thought, *This man I think should be president is asking me what I think?!* I told him Southerners like people who are warm and approachable and that he seemed cold. Needless to say, I was never in a commercial.

Soon after that lost election, I decided the Democratic Party was not for me, and I started looking for a place to fit in. It was then I decided that the Democratic Party leaders didn't have a clue what average people thought. Of course, I believe this is still true today.

A bit later I got divorced and was living alone for the first time in my adult life. I was mowing the lawn, fixing things, and trying to become self-sufficient. I was feeling like a loser because of my failed marriage. I guess I was as far down as I could be and still get up. I never really believed in "being saved." I had attended church all my life. I had gone through baptism, catechism, and was president of the Luther League (a high school youth group) at my church. I knew I was a Christian, but there came a moment when I *felt* the presence of God. I felt God telling me that if I could come to Him and turn my life over to Him, not only would I be saved, I would be able to handle the ups and downs of my life with grace. I can describe the feeling of that moment only as the peace of the presence of God. Since then, when I make God the center, my life is easy, and when I don't, it's chaotic. It is hard being a competent, intellectual person because every so often I want to say I can do it better than God can and every time I try to do it alone, God reminds me that I can't. Accepting Him gave me peace, grace, forgiveness, and a feeling of divine presence that cannot be explained through anything other than the existence of God.

Over the next year and a half, I reconnected with and married my college sweetheart. I was too busy to think much about politics. After we married, I instantly became a stay-at-home mother of three boys. By the middle of the next year, I had a cancer scare (easily treated because it was caught early) and then was pregnant with my daughter, our fourth child. Just thinking about the pace of my life back then makes me tired. About six weeks into my pregnancy, my doctor did the first sonogram. In 1991, the pictures were still grainy and hard to make out, but I could hear the heartbeat and see that big bright beating heart in that little tadpole of a baby. That was the other defining moment of my conversion to conservatism: I was looking at that bright beating heart, and I knew I had been wrong all my life about abortion. I thanked God for never having to make that "choice."

In 1992, I began listening to talk radio. I listened to a local show on WDUN AM 550 called *Morning Talk* and to Rush Limbaugh in the afternoons. One day, during the early days of the 1992 presidential campaign, I watched *60 Minutes* and heard Hillary Clinton disparage stay-at-home moms with her infamous statement, "I could have just stayed home and baked cookies." This smug, elitist statement forever separated *us* from *them*. It confirmed in one statement what Democrats really thought of average Americans. They really do believe the average American, left to their own devices, can't make good decisions on their own, that the liberal elites know what is best for all of us. But those of us coming from the center-right majority were the ones who made it through feminism and the sexual revolution and began to question what it was all about. So how did I respond to that? I placed a call to my conservative friend, talk radio.

I made my first call to talk radio as a result of Hillary Clinton's "cookie" remark. After calling in for a while to WDUN AM 550 in Gainesville, the station invited me to do a few guest segments with Bill Maine. Soon I began doing a show called *Midday* with a woman named E. J. Gore. She was so liberal that debating her every day solidified what I believed. That show didn't last long, but within a couple of years I was hosting my own show, *The Martha Zoller Show*. I would like to say the rest was a piece of cake, but that would be a lie. As with everything worth having, I had to work for it.

When I went back to work, my main priority was that my family wouldn't suffer. Working at WDUN for the Jacobs family was the perfect fit. We had an understanding: I didn't ask for more money and Jay Jacobs didn't ask for more time. I was home when the bus got home, and I was able to have the flexibility I needed. When things would come up, as they always do, there was a family atmosphere at work. Unlike many working mothers, I had help when I needed and that's the way it should work. Over time, I was able to begin doing local TV on a program through Brenau University called *The Brenau News Forum*. Soon, I wanted to branch out into Atlanta TV. When I talked to people they said Fox 5 Atlanta's *The Georgia Gang* was a locally produced show, but they would never consider putting someone like me on the show. I took on the challenge.

I found out all I could about the show, then cleared my schedule for the time they taped. I called Dick Williams, the moderator, once a month. I would say, "You call yourself *The Georgia Gang* and all you are is a bunch of writers from Atlanta. Half of the voters in Georgia are women, and you only have on your show one occasional woman." Finally, he asked around, listened to my radio show, and, in June of 2000, I got my chance. I knew he would love me, and he did.

Eventually I got into a rotation of doing about forty shows a year and serving occasionally as substitute host.

After being seen on *The Georgia Gang* by someone at CNN, I was invited to appear on *Talk Back Live with Bobbie Battista*. *Talk Back Live* was a show produced in Atlanta using several viewer participation methods. Again, I was ready to step in at the last minute with what they considered a new perspective. In reality, my view is a mainstream perspective and that is why it resonates.

After *Talk Back Live*, Bobbie and her producer, Wendy Guarisco, "retired." It was a transition period at CNN and many long time employees like Wendy and Bobbie went on to other projects. Bobbie and Wendy decided that I would become Wendy's project. She needed to get a start in the other side of TV booking business after booking guests on *Talk Back Live* for years, and I needed to be booked on TV. It was a perfect marriage. I stayed prepared and ready when calls came. I am now doing several appearances a month on cable news shows, as well as a full and multifaceted media career. I don't have anyone that rides the bus anymore in my family, but I still make my schedule around them. I have always said, "Women can have it all, just not at the same time."

The mistakes I made up until I was thirty framed my point of view. I took things too seriously; I was too dramatic and undisciplined. I made life-altering mistakes. But then I found my way back to God and let God turn my life into something worthy of the goals I had set for myself long ago. I spent my twenties thinking I knew better than God did. Thankfully, I was given a second chance to use my talents. God was the ultimate elephant in the room of my life, and it is my hope that my mature adult life has reflected the fact that He is invisible to me no more.

Our National Moral Code

Half the battle to solving a problem is identifying it, but too many people stop there. Many only complain about a problem and never offer a solution. In the last ten years we have graduated from the "me generation" that was a product of the decadence of the sexual revolution and are returning to our American origins. America is a conservative country founded on the cornerstone principles and practices of religion. At its beginning and at its foundation, America symbolizes the freedom to find and practice faith. In the face of tragedy, those of us with faith turn to religion, while many of those who never had faith find it or begin to look for it.

The big lesson of the 2004 elections was the resurgence of morals-based voting. There was great wringing of hands among the liberal media over the exit polling that indicated moral issues were the biggest issues in this election. Why the surprise? If a moral code guides your life, it will be the cornerstone of all of your opinions. These voters have always been there in America. They don't usually march or complain because they are busy making ends meet and taking care of their families. But when they are motivated, they vote. And when they vote, Republicans make big gains.

For decades we tried to redefine morality, to make it simply living in honor of one's own conscience and tolerating all ideas. The truth is, morality can't be defined in such a way. Traditional, conservative, faith-based moral values are the foundation of everything Americans believe in. They keep our nation on the right track.

Geraldine Ferraro, the former vice-presidential candidate and Fox News contributor, said if the issues of concern among voters had been the economy, health care, and other domestic issues, Democrats would have won. She was saying the voters who were voting on moral issues weren't voting on those issues. The fact is that morality is the cornerstone of *all* of those issues. How you practice your moral code determines your views on other issues. Like a faith in God, morality can't be separated from your views on any issue.

If political candidates can convey those moral issues to the majority of Americans, then they can win elections. President Clinton co-opted the moral issues-message but without really believing in the values behind the issues. When President Clinton gave his Inaugural Address in 1993, I thought for a moment I might have been wrong about him. But I quickly decided he didn't believe in the values he espoused. Winning was his only goal. Winning is great, but winning without principles is empty. I found it amusing that in the waning days of the 2004 elections, the mantra from the Kerry campaign was around truth and who was telling the truth—this from the same people who didn't care that Clinton lied under oath to the American people, from the same people who changed positions with the political winds. George W. Bush lives these issues and positions and won the people's vote because he believes the values behind the issues. He is a true compassionate conservative who understands the center-right majority.

I am optimistic that in the long run, good wins and evil is defeated. Above all, fairness will win. Of course, the older I get, the more my philosophy is challenged. I understand that compromise has to play a role. There is a power structure that must be respected. However, politicians who know where the line is, who hold on to their ideals and who will stand up for the important things *can* be successful. Three of my favorite politicians had a similar philosophy—Paul Coverdell, Zell Miller, and Phil Gramm. They all governed by the idea that those who are willing to pass on the credit to get some of what they want can look back at the end of a career and know they have done some good work for this nation while upholding its moral ideals.

Indivisible

This book makes the case that we are not as distant on issues as we might think. Americans are forward-thinking people at our best. We know where we are and where we need to go. We all need to spend a little more time learning from the past without dwelling on it. We read about our divided nation, but it doesn't jibe with what we see in our everyday life.

We also need to remember to work together on political issues instead of looking for the first microphone to create a controversy. I say this as an American, not as an analyst. In my work life, I benefit from controversy, but as Americans we need to put the welfare of our country first. We need to recognize the issues that have acted as elephants in the room to our leaders, our media, and our neighbors.

These issues are not new in America. Since our nation's founding, Americans have found themselves trampled by herds of these elephants to the extent that what was once obvious to our founding fathers is considered to be out of the mainstream today. Over time, even the meanings of the American founding principles, obvious to the signers of the Declaration of Independence, have slowly eroded. Our nation's founding principles have over time lost any authoritative meaning to the American people. Today those principles are portrayed by the liberal media and Democratic leaders as nothing more than glittering prose from a bygone era, as ideals impossible to live by. The authority understood to emanate from America's founding principles has been supplanted over time by other principles from other sources and various societal concerns that demonstrate no real source of authority.

The clearest example of this is the *Roe v. Wade* decision and the so-called "right to privacy." There is nothing in the Declaration of Independence of the United States that discusses privacy as a right. As *Plessy v. Ferguson* was overturned by *Brown v. Board of Education*, *Roe v. Wade* will be overtuned also, in time. Let us hope for the sake of about 1.3 million unborn children that this is sooner rather than later. This is an issue that should be left up to the states.

The founders' expressions are clear. Even a casual reading of the Declaration of Independence invites the reader to contemplate a sense of meaning larger than life as we know it, larger than words can express. Yet over the generations, the obvious meaning with which Thomas Jefferson infused America's founding document seems to have gone into hiding.

The faith and belief that middle America is the true mainstream led me to write *Indivisible*. It is the grown-up protesters longing for the "good ol' days" of the 1960s who are out of the mainstream. Wesley Clark was an analyst for CNN (though now with Fox News) and a former NATO Supreme Allied Commander in the Clinton administration. In 2003, he participated in a fundraiser I was doing for the Freedom Alliance Scholarship Fund with a call-in interview. I asked him why the Democratic Party was not trusted by the American people on national security, defense, and terrorism issues.

He said the party had been hijacked by the Vietnam anti-war movement and if he decided to run as a Democrat (which he did), he wanted to bring back some credibility to the party on those issues.

Zell Miller said basically the same things in his book *A National Party No More* and during his keynote address at the Republican National Convention in 2004 and was chastised by his own party. But Zell Miller and General Clark had it right, though Clark changed his view in order to have a future in the upper ranks of the Democratic Party. The party of John F. Kennedy has lost its way. Instead of being the party of the people, they have become the party of the special interest groups, knitted together by such a tenuous alliance that it will be difficult for them ever to win a national election again.

By the time you finish this book, I hope you will see what many liberals don't want you to see—that we have more that unites us than divides us. The politicians who can capitalize on that and have the more optimistic, moral message, like Ronald Reagan, will win. President George W. Bush understands that, too. He sees our nation for what it is . . . one nation . . . under God . . . indivisible. When the votes were counted, for the first time in fifteen years we could tell Americans see it too. We have more to unite us than to divide us.

The American Foundation

As I considered the writing of this book, I knew that I believed the foundation concepts of our republic to be key . . . not only to the framework of this book but to the framework of the American nation. In 2005 we saw battles between Democrats and Republicans over judicial nominees and the appropriateness of the filibuster. As this year becomes next, we'll witness these issues come to the surface again over President Bush's nominations to fill the Supreme Court seats vacated by the retirement of Justice Sandra Day O'Connor and the death of Chief Justice William Rehnquist. In these days of judicial activism, a clear understanding of the tenets, the very foundation, of American society will prove essential to our very survival.

We must do better in understanding the important words laid down in our national documents by the founding fathers. They are as important today as they were then. It is also important that we recognize the power a president's words have had and continue to have to motivate and guide us, to mold our character as a people. We must also be ever aware of the political party process and how it came to be. These are not just things that happened and they are not things that can be changed just because they seem outdated. In a true study of our republic, the concepts and ideas of the founders will never be outdated.

CHAPTER ONE

The Declaration of Independence: America's Founding Principles

We hold these truths to be self-evident, that all men are created equal, that they are endowed by their Creator with certain unalienable Rights, that among these are Life, Liberty and the pursuit of Happiness.
    —The Declaration of Independence, signed July 4, 1776

The top of the hour introduction for *The Martha Zoller Show* includes a medley of several American themes, one of which is a recitation of these first few lines of the Declaration of Independence. I lead off each hour that way for a reason. I believe it is vital that Americans hear those words repeated often. The Declaration of Independence is much more than a simple declaration of sovereignty for the American nation; it is statement of what we *are*. The document is the foundation of our rights as American citizens, but a revelation of the source of human rights for *all* people. We should be reminded every day—if not even at the top of every hour—of this blessing.

It is inescapable that if human rights exist at all, they exist by virtue of a gift by God at the moment of human creation. In other words, human rights are a birthright, given to us by our Creator. The Declaration of Independence documents that truth. Our founders thought the truth of inalienable rights was "self-evident" and said as much.

"We Hold These Truths to Be Self-Evident"

Some people may disagree by claiming the Constitution is the document that gives (or "sources") us these rights. But a reading of the Constitution indicates no actual source of human rights. The Constitution only secures and protects human rights sourced within the rationale of principles found in the Declaration of Independence. Although it is true that the Constitution specifically enumerates some of the various human rights, the 9th Amendment makes it clear those rights were established before the Constitution came into being:

> The enumeration in the Constitution, of certain rights, shall not be construed to deny or disparage others retained by the people.

Because those other rights are "retained by the people," they must have been placed with the people prior to the Constitution. In 1787, via their authorized representatives, the American people chose to assign to a federal government certain restricted authority. The ability for the people to do so sprang from the Declaration's principle of unalienable rights. Thus, the major purpose of the Constitution is to enumerate the restricted authority "we the people" allocate to our federal government.

Of course there are those who will point out that human rights exist in many other nations of the world. The freedoms we hold in this country are not the provenance of America alone. They will follow up by saying that because human rights exist outside of America, those rights must have an establishment or cause outside of their historically unique American context. Those people will unwittingly help to make my point.

Self-governing republics of the world, those nations whose decisions are made by the people indirectly through representative government, derive authority from the people. We must not forget that, for the people of a nation to ratify a constitution, those people must themselves possess sufficient rightful authority. That authority had to come to them from some source. Logic dictates that human rights cannot exist prior to human existence. That being true, then where might the authority sufficient for humans to agree on a constitution come from if not from some source in existence prior to their own? After all, unless human rights are endowed to each of us at least by the time of our birth, and then later put to work to, among other things, authorize constitutions, then even self-governing, constitutional republics can demonstrate no valid source of authority.

An analysis of the Declaration's expressions establishes that those who signed it on July 4, 1776, understood it carried the sum total of all sovereign authority of the American nation. From the point of that signing, the United States of America was a viable nation with sufficient sovereign authority to fight a war and carry out its essential business. Over that time, the nation's business transpired solely with the use of the authority that sprang from the Declaration of Independence. The Declaration's authority was first put to use to empower the Articles of Confederation in 1777. Ten years later, in 1787, that same authority sanctioned a newly proposed Constitution of the United States and empowered that document when the supreme law was ratified by the states on the first Wednesday in March 1789. So without the Declaration of Independence documenting a new source of American sovereign authority, as it first did in 1776, any new constitution written subsequent to that date would have no source of authority. The Declaration, which begins with a statement of the freedoms and powers given by God, is the foundation of the Articles of Confederation, the original Constitution of the United States and all of its subsequent amendments. All these documents—and by historical association the very existence of this great country—depend directly on the authority that springs from the expression of God-given freedoms in the Declaration of Independence.

"The Laws of Nature and Nature's God"

The Declaration of Independence did what its name suggests by declaring the independence of the union of "free and independent states." The founders, however, did not stop at merely declaring independence. Our founding document indicates that American sovereignty is actually a logical conclusion resulting from a chosen rationale of principles. Because the American sovereign authority is the result of reasoning, the truth and integrity of those reasons is vital for the continued sovereignty of our nation.

The founders had at their disposal any number of tools from which to choose to secure a declaration of sovereign authority. For example, they could have simply stated their new nation's independence in the form of a straightforward resolution with no further justification. They could have formulated a case that the American people simply didn't care for the rule by the king of England so they chose to abolish it and create a new set of national rules they might like better. The American founders did neither of these. Instead they formulated a specific rationale to justify their declaration. That rationale involves several principles, one of which documents the giver or "source" of all human rights in the world. That rationale begins by conveying the following:

> When in the Course of human events, it becomes necessary for one people to dissolve the Political Bands which have connected them with another, and to assume among the Powers of the Earth, the separate and equal Station to which the Laws of Nature and of Nature's God entitle them, a decent Respect to the Opinions of Mankind requires that they should declare the causes which impel them to the Separation.

So, according to the Declaration, it was "the laws of nature and nature's God" that entitled the colonists to "break the political bands" with England. American authority is rigidly coupled with the "self-evident truth" of God and God's laws. Thus, according to the founding fathers, there can be no American sovereign authority without God and God's laws. They believed the United States of America was a special place coming to fruition at a special time for God's special purpose. It is important for Americans today to understand and believe that, as long as they are adhering to God's law and encouraging modern day America to do so as well, the United States can continue to feel the freedoms provided by God's blessing.

Reading further, we discover those "laws of nature and nature's God" are none other than the following self-evident truths:

that all men are created equal;

that they are endowed by their Creator with certain unalienable rights;

that among these are life, liberty, and the pursuit of happiness;

that to secure these rights, governments are instituted among men, deriving their just powers from the consent of the governed;

that whenever any form of government becomes destructive of these ends, it is the right of the people to alter or to abolish it, and to institute new government, laying its foundation on such principles and organizing its powers in such form, as to them shall seem most likely to effect their safety and happiness.

Even though the loose confederation of states that adopted the Declaration of Independence often falls short of the lofty goals set out by the Declaration, the foundation for these goals was created by the Declaration. Having declared that equality among men and human rights are self-evident truth and having declared that God, the creator of all things, endows those rights at the moment of human creation, the founders followed with the truth that the primary purpose of government is to secure those God-given rights. The founders then reasoned that, if any such a government should become sufficiently destructive of those rights, it would be the right of the people to alter or to abolish that government, and to institute a new government. This logical and simple understanding of basic rights is what allows this republic to remain strong. Once taken apart and analyzed, the Declaration of Independence is probably one of the greatest and most effective documents of its kind in human history. It is that simplicity and foundation in God that provides the obvious solution to all the issues in our country. We need to look no further than this founding document, in tandem with the Constitution, to guide us.

"From the Consent of the Governed"

The signers of the Declaration specifically authorized their successors to convene and write a constitution for the purpose of instituting a new national government. That authority is derived from the principle in the Declaration that states the following:

> That to secure these [human] Rights, Governments are instituted among Men, deriving their just Powers from the Consent of the Governed.

The founders authorized their successors to pursue actions in keeping with that authoritative truth. Thus the people's representatives who convened to write the Constitution of the United States counted on this principle to establish a national government. Within the logic of that principle resides the sole source of authority for the United States federal government.

Furthermore, because the Constitution states no source of authority beyond "We the People of the United States," and because the United States of America draws its authority from the principles of the Declaration of Independence, the Constitution depends directly upon those principles for its authority. If any one principle in the Declaration of Independence could be proven false, the philosophical validity of our national government would cease to exist.

It is important that the founders announced their own source of authority as they made their declaration to the world. In their conclusion, they stated plainly that they acted with "the Authority of the good People of these Colonies." Only the people, in expression of the rights "endowed by their Creator," possessed such authority. The founders themselves possessed only personal authority. Any declaration they might make using their own personal authority would be null and void. But because the people of the colonies were endowed at birth with the authority to "alter or abolish" any government that sufficiently destroyed their rights, and because those people authorized the founders to represent them at the Second Continental Congress, the founders certified within the Declaration of Independence that they acted authoritatively.

"On the Protection of Divine Providence"

After stating the several "truthful" principles, those being the "laws of nature and nature's God," the founders offered evidence to the world that the government under the king of England had become sufficiently destructive of the colonists' human rights, enough so to trigger actions associated with the last principle of their rationale. That principle allows the people to "alter or abolish" a government and "institute a new government." After establishing that all the rights come from the "Supreme Judge of the world," the founders issued what is nothing more than a simple logical conclusion to their rationale of principles and stated evidence.

> We, therefore, the Representatives of the UNITED STATES OF AMERICA, in General Congress, Assembled, appealing to the Supreme Judge of the World for the Rectitude of our Intentions, do, in the Name, and by the Authority of the good People of these Colonies, solemnly Publish and Declare, That these United Colonies are, and of Right ought to be Free and Independent States; that they are absolved from all Allegiance to the British Crown, and that all political Connection between them and the State of Great Britain, is and ought to be totally dissolved; and that as Free and Independent States, they have full Power to levy War, conclude Peace, contract Alliances, establish Commerce, and to do all other Acts and Things which Independent States may of right do. And for the support of this Declaration, with a firm Reliance on the Protection of divine Providence, we mutually pledge to each other our lives, our Fortunes and our sacred Honor.

In the study of the Declaration of Independence, many wonder why the founders used such a complicated language to declare the simple nature of America's sovereignty. It was not because it was the prose of the day; it was because it was evident to these new Americans that without a clear and undeniable discussion of where our rights come from, then government may trample the rights of the people. What many in government today forget is that their authority depends on the premise that human rights are "unalienable." By using that circular logic, our founders ensured no tool of government, using the sovereign authority reasoned to exist on July 4th, 1776, could ever rightfully deny the people their rights. That is what the principles of the Declaration of Independence are all about—protecting human rights and God-given freedoms. When you understand the founders' logic, the purpose behind the principles of America becomes obvious.

The American nation was created where sovereign authority depends upon the reality that human rights exist by virtue of endowment by God. The Founders defined the primary role of this new nation's government to secure those God-given rights. If this new form of government could successfully secure God's gift to mankind, the founders reasoned that God would be pleased with their new nation. They also reasoned that God would provide their new nation divine protection.

We might call this idea the "Theory of America." The founders created the United States of America to test the theory that an earthly nation of people guided by certain exalted principles would be protected by divine Providence. We, the citizens of America, continue today to play a part in this grand experiment of the founders of this great nation.

In his farewell address to the nation, George Washington, confirmed the theoretical nature of the American nation as he urged all future generations of Americans to:

> Observe good faith and justice towards all Nations; cultivate peace and harmony with all. Religion and Morality enjoin this conduct; and can it be, that good policy does not equally enjoin it? It will be

worthy of a free, enlightened, and, at no distant period, a great Nation, to give to mankind the magnanimous and too novel example of a people always guided by an exalted justice and benevolence. Who can doubt, that, in the course of time and things, the fruits of such a plan would richly repay any temporary advantages, which might be lost by a steady adherence to it? Can it be, that Providence has not connected the permanent felicity of a Nation with its Virtue? The experiment, at least, is recommended by every sentiment which ennobles human nature.

George Washington believed the United States of America was formed as an experiment to test whether Providence has connected a nation's permanence with its virtue. The America nation was designed to do God's will, as its citizens understand it. To do so would be "virtuous." So, according to that theory, a virtuous nation should enjoy "permanent felicity." Abraham Lincoln understood the American Theory and years later echoed Washington's remarks when he urged the crowd at the Cooper Union Institute to "have faith that right makes might, and in that faith, let us, to the end, dare to do our duty as we understand it."

The idea "right makes might" is simply another way of expressing the American Theory. Accordingly, God empowers and protects those who do His will. To anyone who believes in the goodness of God, that should seem obvious. Lincoln urged Americans to "dare to do their duty" and to demonstrate faith by acting on their belief that "right makes might."

Separation of Church and State?

Many people will say the world has changed too much and the phrases used in the Declaration, the Constitution, and the quaint, patriotic speeches of presidents past were made by men who did not live in the kind of world we live in. Foundations don't change. People still want to provide for their families without government interference, and they still want the opportunity to work and show what they can do for themselves. They still want to hold to the truth that God is on their side. We still have an overwhelming need to do what is right in God's eyes. If not, then why did many people, even those who said they weren't sure if they believed in God, turn to churches after the 9/11 attacks?

I will never forget an interview I watched with a man who had lost his mother. He was going to church and was asked if he was a religious person. He said he wasn't, but he had a need to turn to God to help him deal with his grief. He knew it was what his mother would want him to do. It is a feeling in the soul of every person on earth, to turn to a higher power in times of crisis.

If America's sovereign authority is charged with the responsibility to do God's will, as we all long to do, then why do so many claim a "separation between church and state" in our Constitution? There is actually nothing in the Constitution about such a separation. Those who make this argument make a hollow one. The Constitution merely restricts Congress from using its power to establish a state-run religion.

Those who long to declare a separation between church and state mistakenly import into the constitutional language a letter written by Thomas Jefferson years after the Constitution was ratified. The context of that letter indicates Jefferson conveyed much the same message we see in the First Amendment. However, he chose, regrettably, to phrase his concerns by using the words "separation between church and state." Even so, those words carry no constitutional authority, regardless of the way individuals choose to interpret them. Jefferson only rendered a personal opinion when he penned that letter, not an interpretation of the Constitution or the Declaration of Independence.

Mark Levin's *Men in Black: How the Supreme Court is Destroying America* reminds us of the history behind the more recent use of that phrase. In 1947, the case of *Everson v. Board of Education* changed the balance between government and religion, Justice Hugo Black used the "separation of church and state" phrase from the letter Jefferson wrote to a Baptist community in Danbury, Connecticut. Black used the phrase to create the illusion of the "wall of separation" and expanded the First Amendment of the Constitution (which was meant to protect the people from Federal intrusion into the practice of religion) to states and local governments. While the decision in the case did protect the fair treatment of religion in the public square, parts of Black's opinion became the rallying point for the anti-religious precedent that has mounted an assault on religious freedom in this country today.

According to the founders, God is not a religious belief, but rather a "self-evident truth." Because God is truth, truth on which our nation's authority depends, there is no connection between the founders' expressions in the Declaration of Independence and organized religion. God is an assumed truth in the founders' declaration. Because the actual declaration of sovereign authority for the United States of America depends upon the truth that God exists, the only way the sovereignty of this nation can be denied is through the proof that God does not exist.

Whether Americans believe in the American principles is debatable. To the extent that Americans do believe in those principles, and because those principles formulate a religious doctrine for those who believe in them, the American principles provide a valid religious framework for Americans to consider. Lincoln once even referred to this concept as a "political religion." He urged Americans to accept that religious doctrine. While Americans are free to believe what they wish, the various tools of American government have no choice but to respect the truth of God's existence. According to our founding document, God's authority first flows through individual citizens, eventually to find its way to our government. So if God does not exist, neither humans nor governments can possess any authority. A world without God is therefore the definition of anarchy. A study of the history of mankind demonstrates the truth of that statement.

That the founding fathers personally fell short of the goals they laid out in the Declaration of Independence, the Constitution, and the formation of this republic does not mean the goals are not worth fighting for. In one of Condoleezza Rice's first interviews after becoming Secretary of State, she commented about Thomas Jefferson's personal failure to live up to his ideals. America is about aiming high, and there is no greater model for this notion than the lofty ideals of the founding fathers despite their personal failings.

There are many affronts to the First Amendment today, but they are not coming from the Right. It seems the Left, which once stood for freedom of speech, now wants to limit governmental speech referring to God. Of recent concern to the liberal deniers of free expression is the American motto "In God We Trust." Those words are inscribed on each item of currency our government prints or mints. Of course there are those who claim that by doing so our government endorses religion. They claim—wrongly, of course—that such an endorsement is contrary to a constitutional requirement of a separation of church and state.

In reality, our national motto has no religious connotation whatsoever, but is instead a simple statement of historical fact about the foundation of this nation. Our founders, having elicited the necessary authority to do so, placed trust in God to provide America with divine protection. They did so as the necessary justification to declare American sovereignty. They understood they were taking great risks by breaking the political bonds with Great Britain. They "firmly relied on the protection of divine Providence" to support them. They trusted God that they would not fail and used the authority elicited from the American people. Plainly, the founders felt that "In God We Trust."

Also of issue to liberals is the Pledge of Allegiance. According to our founding document, America is actually "one nation under God." Within the expressions of that document, America's sovereign authority is assigned with the task of defending God's endowment of human rights on earth. In exchange, God would provide the new nation protection. Since God has the power sufficient to protect America, and because the founders solicited that protection as a condition for our nation's existence, America is "one nation under [God's]" care. That's all our pledge says. Because the pledge simply states that fact, the words carry no implicit statement of religious belief or intent. Again, religions deal with present spiritual beliefs, not historical ones.

The American Democracy

Finally, I'd like to speak briefly to the idea that America is a democracy. I'll speak more specifically to this notion in the next chapter, but at this time, let me draw a few distinctions. A democracy is a nation whose authority springs from the opinions of its people. A democracy is designed to make its decisions by polling its citizens, adding up the votes, and acting on the opinion of the majority. In short, a democracy is a nation ruled by public opinion. Those opinions may be good or bad, ethical or unethical, right or wrong. Either way, in a democracy public opinions are authoritative.

America is different than a democracy in one vital respect. America's sovereign authority springs not from public opinion, but from certain exalted principles detailed in the Declaration of Independence. Certainly public opinion has much to do with the manner in which our nation makes its decisions; however, public opinion in and of itself carries no actual authority unless those opinions are grounded in our founding principles. Much in the manner that curbs on the sides of our roads help us to drive where we are authorized, our founding principles guide the direction of our country. America's founding principles provide the authoritative framework within which our nation's decisions must be made.

Because our founding principles are our nation's source of authority, and because America is not authorized to violate those principles, our founding principles help us to stay "between the lines," so to speak. In that manner, America's founding principles help keep our nation pointed in the right direction—regardless of transient prevailing popular opinions.

In addition, according to our founders' declaration, only the "Supreme Judge of the world" is the final judge as to whether our nation stays between the lines. This is the founders' model. This is why America is not truly a democracy. This is also why America is not simply another nation among nations. This is why people who live in America are the most fortunate people on earth.

Our great fortune, however, implies an obligation to help secure human rights to those whose rights are consistently violated.

According to the Declaration of Independence, a nation's sovereign authority depends upon respecting God's endowment of human rights. Therefore, no nation has sufficient authority to trample its citizens' human rights. Along with rights come responsibilities. Because our government's primary purpose is to secure human rights, and because "all men are created equal," our Declaration of Independence assigns our nation and its government the responsibility to do what we can to secure those same rights and freedoms for people in other nations of the world. This is our nation's calling. Protecting human rights is what our nation's authority is defined and designed to do. So say our founding principles.

CHAPTER TWO

And to the Republic,
for Which It Stands

Today I advocate the restoration of the American republic. . . . The qualities of the republic are related to each other and to the realities of our age. A spirit of citizen duty and participation is required to guarantee the sovereignty of the people. When citizens abdicate their duties, they are no longer sovereign.
—Gary Hart, Former Senator and Presidential Candidate,
February 2003

Something happened in the late 1950s—politicians started regularly referring to the United States of America as a *democracy* rather than a *republic*. That subtle change was in many ways what began the downward spiral of the understanding of our founding principles. The United States of America is a democratic republic. We vote and believe in the rights of the majority, but we also protect the rights of the individual.

In 1992, third party candidate Ross Perot wanted to take us to a sort of virtual democracy with his idea of town hall meetings to decide every major issue. On the surface, it sounds like a good idea. Let the will of the people rule. But our form of government protects both the rights of the majority and the rights of the individual. Thankfully so, because it protects us from our darker instincts like slavery or the limitation of the right to vote. If we were a democracy, there would have never been a Civil Rights Act or a Voting Rights Act, for instance.

However, in such a republic where the rights of the individual are protected against the potentially unjust will of the majority, there is always the danger of the rights of the individual *infringing* on the rights of the majority. It is a delicate balance. I believe we are out of balance now when it comes to the rights of the overwhelmingly Christian majority in this country. But I believe in the ability of the scales of American justice to gain back the proper balance. I believe in what I call "the American pendulum" to swing back in favor of the rightful moral majority.

A Jeffersonian Democracy

While it is true that most European leaders today do not understand America's sense of authority in the world, most Americans do not either. Most Americans do not understand the authoritative nature of American principles because they don't understand the nature of our history. Every day Americans have an opportunity to live up to the ideals of our country's founders. We have the opportunity to wake up each day and start over with the goals that the One who has given us those rights and that authority has for us.

I've already addressed the incorrect notion that America's form of government is a democracy in the classic sense, that it is instead a democratic republic. According to Article IV, Section VI of the U.S. Constitution:

> The United States shall guarantee to every State in this Union a Republican Form of Government, and shall protect each of them against Invasion; and on Application of the Legislature, or of the Executive (when the Legislature cannot be convened) against domestic Violence.

The importance of this section of our Constitution cannot be overemphasized. In fact, Abraham Lincoln used this reference in our

Constitution to justify his decision to use force against the rebelling states in the spring of 1861. This section of our Constitution is the glue that requires the American states to remain intact. This section requires each state to operate within what is called a "republican" form of government.

Pundits and politicians throw terms like "republican" and "democrat" around fairly loosely and with very little thought as to what their classical meaning might be. Many people think a "democracy" is a "republic" and vice versa. A republican government's authority flows to it from the people (or public). Generally speaking, the people are represented in the various layers of the government by those of their choosing. In the classic sense, each individual in a republican government is authorized to govern himself, as a part of the overall government. Individuals, governing themselves, are the basic building blocks of a republican government.

However, individuals in a republic solely govern themselves only up to the point at which they become no longer, as Thomas Jefferson put it, "competent" to do so. At that point, those individuals elect representatives to make decisions for them. The public is thereby represented by others on all those matters for which they possess no competence to represent themselves. Thus "republican" is defined as a representative of and for the public.

But what did Thomas Jefferson mean by the term "competence"? Let's say you are a farmer, your neighbor down the road is a lawyer, and your friend in town is a grocer. Each of you is in charge of governing yourself and your own actions; you are self-governing. Each of you possesses the personal authority to do so, endowed to you at creation by God. Each of you has certain specific interests that don't involve the other members of your group, like the education and welfare of your children. Those are the interests over which you maintain direct control. In Jefferson's vernacular, those things over which you maintain direct control should be those you are "competent" to govern.

But those things over which you possess only a partial interest and thereby only a partial right to control, you are not "competent" to govern. For example, a road is for the greater good. However, you, singly, cannot make the final decision on where the road will go. While you have interest in the road, that interest is not solely yours to control.

So you and your lawyer and grocer neighbors down the road agree to elect someone to represent you to make all those decisions that affect the group. Each of you agrees to transfer enough personal authority to the group's representative so he or she is fully authorized to make the group's decisions. As each succeeding layer of decision-making surpasses the "competence" of that layer's elected representative, those representatives agree to elect even higher-level representatives to make the decisions for the groups they represent.

Republicanism merely refers to the *structure* of government. Republicanism has nothing to do with ideology or the criteria for decision-making, only *who* is authorized to make decisions.

Competence has another application as well. Jefferson wrote, "A democracy [is] the only pure republic, but impracticable beyond the limits of a town." The author of the Declaration of Independence understood that a democracy is simply a certain type of republic, one that allows for individuals to represent themselves and societal decisions to be made by majority rule. Jefferson understood that beyond the limits of a "town," individuals would no longer be "competent" to make direct majority rule decisions on each issue that might come up for a vote. Jefferson recognized the impracticability of direct majority-rule system in which every man's viewpoint would be solicited on each issue.

Most importantly, with respect to "competence," Jefferson understood members of a society the size of Jeffersonian "towns" would have similar viewpoints and opinions. Theoretically, the preferences and opinions of individuals with similar viewpoints and opinions should be similar as well. Jefferson understood that the democratic (that is, direct majority rule) decision-making within a local society ("town") composed of individuals with similar viewpoints and opinions would be a voluntary act to help facilitate action regarding the preferences and opinions of that local society.

On the other hand, Jefferson knew that the democratic decision-making within a global society with dissimilar viewpoints and opinions can easily become an involuntary act of subjugation with respect to the preferences and opinions of certain minority constituencies. He understood that a democracy is impractical from the standpoint of protecting the endowed rights of minorities within any given society. The larger the society, the more pronounced the differences of viewpoints and opinions within any given set of local minorities. At the point a local society is large enough that decisions formulated on majority opinion begin to injure the endowed human rights of local minorities, that Jeffersonian society would reach a theoretical cut-off point for making democratic decisions. That's because no individual or group has sufficient authority to deny to another certain endowed human rights. Jefferson understood further enlargement of a society would no doubt foster egregious treatment of minorities' rights by the majority.

Jefferson believed America would eventually become a nation of Jeffersonian "towns." The townsfolk would have similar needs and desires. Within Jeffersonian communities, individuals would to work together in a common fashion, voting and committing local resources for community projects and programs in a democratic fashion. Those projects and programs would be financed locally, and the benefits would accrue for the use of all community members equally. At a local level, Jefferson's ideal governmental structure would approximate a democracy—a "Jeffersonian democracy."

The General Welfare

Considered by Jefferson in the conceptual framework of his ideal local democracy is the theory of "the general welfare." Within any particular local democratic society, the theory of democratic decision-making allows for all participants to have the opportunity to directly benefit from that society's decisions. Democratic societies are theoretically small enough that the welfare of each citizen can be affected positively by local societal decisions, whether those decisions might concern water systems, school systems, roads, or services that might emanate from the local governmental entity. In any particular local democratic society, those relatively few individuals who perceive no direct benefit from local democratic decisions still have alternatives. Individuals can always decide to move to other local democracies that might make decisions according to criteria more agreeable to their particular lifestyles and concerns. In such a manner, the welfare of each citizen is taken into consideration by local decisions arrived at "democratically." Thus Jeffersonian democracies provide for "the general welfare" of all citizens.

As the size of local society enlarges, there comes a point at which certain local minorities have very little choice but to succumb to the wishes of the majority. As that local democracy becomes the size of a nation such as the United States of America, there can be no escape for a downtrodden minority. At the point in which a minority constituency is allowed no escape, the majority wields the power necessary to enslave it. This is the societal dynamic that allowed slavery to exist in America. Slavery can only exist in an otherwise free political system when a majority wields the power great enough to subjugate a minority to a state of bondage. The lesson Jefferson wished to convey to us all by his remark is that, without the free and sanctioned practice of democratic decision-making in America, slavery could never have existed. That is because, in a democracy, there is no effective check on the authoritative power of the majority. This is one good reason America was not designed to be a democracy, but instead a democratic republic or Jeffersonian democracy.

The Falsehood of British Democracy

Ironically, our closest freedom-loving ally, Great Britain, is not really a democracy or a republic. Great Britain operates a parliamentary "quasi-democratic" form of government. Unlike in our own system, Great Britain's national authority does not spring from its people. Yes, it is true the British people elect representatives to the House of Commons. And yes, that house of parliament holds the power to make British law. But it still remains that the British system, unlike its American counterpart, does not exist by virtue of any flow of authority from the British people to their representatives.

I must confess, the British royalty fascinates me. I love to watch the pageantry of an official royal ceremony; I remember being glued to the television when Diana married Prince Charles. Likewise, I did the same thing again during Princess Diana's funeral in 1997. My brother-in-law had to travel to London the week after the funeral. When he came into view of Kensington Palace and saw the outpouring of affection for Diana, he was moved to tears.

Although many of us love to watch the royal pomp and circumstance, we as Americans can't help but wonder why the British people subject themselves to it. If nothing else, the British people pay an exorbitant cost to maintain the royal family. From time to time, I hear various British pundits discuss abolishing the British Crown; however, that idea never really gains much support. So what is it about Great Britain that keeps it supporting a royal family in the manner it does, but at the same time operating like a democracy?

The main reason Great Britain will never abolish its royal family is quite simple—*it can't*. The way the British system has evolved, the people of Great Britain have no authority to abolish the royal family and its burden on the national treasury. That's because all British sovereign authority flows through the monarchy. Although Britain operates in many respects like a parliamentary democracy, its basic form of government remains a monarchy run by the monarchy's chosen government.

Within the British system of sovereign authority, all authority originates with God. However, it first passes through the Royal Family and then to the British Lordship on its way to the House of Commons. The House of Commons "allows" its members to be elected by popular opinion. The House of Commons really doesn't have to do that except, if it didn't, there may be rioting in Great Britain.

In fact, riotous activities are what brought about this British system in the first place. Since medieval times, authority was wrested little by little from the British royalty. First, the British lords commanded authority. Subsequently, those known as "commoners" wrested certain authority from the lordships. At each stage at which authority was taken from its previous holder, it was transferred so by agreement—by contract, rather than, say, by decapitation or something equally uncivilized. I suppose those agreements really were among the first "civilized" acts of western mankind.

The first such contract we know as the Magna Carta (or Magna Charta). That contract and all its successors constitute the "British Constitution." According to that series of agreements, the House of Commons is "allowed" to make all the rules in Great Britain. The monarchy agreed to that in the face of uprising. The House of Lords, theoretically superior to the House of Commons, merely interprets the rules set forth by the latter. The House of Lords can be likened to our own Supreme Court. In exchange for the authority given by the monarchy to the various houses, those houses agreed to support the British monarchy. So abolishing the British Crown would violate the set of agreements (the British "Constitution") between the "houses" and the British monarchy.

Because British authority first flows through the monarchy before it arrives at the House of Commons, the House of Commons really has no authority to abolish the royalty. Because the House of Commons has no authority that did not first flow through the monarchy, to abolish the royalty would at the same time abolish the authority necessary to do so. So there they are. Only a people's revolution, similar to that conducted by the American people during the American Revolutionary War, could establish a new flow of sovereign authority bypassing the monarchy in Great Britain. That won't happen as long as the British royal family behaves in a manner the British people expect and respect of them.

Respect of the citizens of Great Britain is vitally important to the monarchy. One way to earn and retain that respect is to behave like royalty. That's one reason for all the pomp and circumstance. The British people expect that from the royal family. To do otherwise would dash their and the world's expectations and bring shame, not only to the British royalty, but also to the British people. After all, the British people support the monarchy in every respect. If members of the monarchy bring shame to themselves, worldwide respect for the British people would diminish.

Great Britain still holds to the "Divine right of kings" model of sovereign authority. In such a system, all authority flows from God; however, it first passes through a monarchy and the monarchy's government before certain residual authority finds its way to the people.

By agreement with the Crown, the British House of Commons has unlimited authority to make law within the British system. Because that house of parliament is directly elected by popular vote, the only remedy for unpopular law is for the people to vote unpopular lawmakers out of office. Their hope can be that new lawmakers will be more popular. Therefore, as British popular opinions change, so one might expect their laws to follow in order to reflect those new opinions. In that manner, the British system of laws allows for the direct input of unbridled popular opinion. Because of this direct input, there is no effective check on the law-making power of the majority opinion.

Nowhere in the British system of governing is the power of the majority necessarily guided by any particular set of rightful principles. That being the case, there are no standards beyond the opinions of the people to judge the merits of any particular law. Because the British law-making system allows for such direct input of the people's opinions, the British system of government, as it has evolved, is designed to do what the majority dictates. As a result, if the majority prefers the government to secure health insurance for its people, then that's what it must do. Because resources are scarce, other functions that do not command as much support from the people necessarily fall to a day when resources are not so scarce.

The American Difference

The governments of Britain and many other civilized democracies of the Western world base their decisions on societal preferences, not authoritative principles. This is where any similarity between the governmental authority of the Western democracies and that of the United States of America ends. America's authority springs from certain rightful principles outlined in the Declaration of Independence.

Those principles are "rightful" because they are the "laws of nature and of nature's God."

The assumption here of course is that the "laws of God" can only be "rightful." The nature and extent of the American authority has in no way changed since American independence was declared. Therefore, the use of American governmental authority must follow authoritative principles, not societal preferences. One of those authoritative principles is that governments are instituted among men to secure God-given human rights. America's authority comes from the principle (among others) that unalienable rights must be satisfied before societal preferences may lay claim to our government's scarce resources. In short, the American authority is designed to secure human rights first, health insurance later. Once the assignment of securing human rights is substantially complete, America might decide to divert the resulting "peace dividend" from that project to others, perhaps to that of insuring the health of its citizens. But as long as resources are scarce, and as long as the task of securing human rights is not complete, the first assignment of American governing authority must be to secure unalienable rights.

Furthermore, because of the principle "all men are created equal," part of our government's assignment entails helping, to the extent that our government's resources will allow, other peoples of the world, downtrodden by despots, to claim their own endowment of God-given human rights and freedoms. That assignment requires American authority to prepare a substantial military to be used to fight, among other causes, the global war on terrorism. American authority is mandated to plant freedom in parts of the world to choke out forces that endanger human rights. Doing so not only helps the peoples of those countries, but also helps to make Americans rights more secure, the assumption being that a free society is far less a danger to its neighbors than a society ruled by despots.

We saw two great examples of progress on that front with the success of the elections in Afghanistan and Iraq. Before the elections, those who would seek to minimize the authority of the people were in power. In both cases, facing life-threatening danger, people went to vote in high numbers. People know they are not free, even though they have never known freedom. People believe life will be better if they control their own destiny. I find it amazing that some people in Iraq walked thirteen miles to get to cast their vote, yet there are people in my own state of Georgia who whine that being asked to show a simple ID card with their picture on it is an infringement on their civil rights. As Sen. John McCain said after the 2000 election, "We are promised free and fair elections, not perfect ones."

The Example of America

Today, there is a great deal of hand-wringing about what the "civilized" peoples of the world (meaning Western Europe) think of us. Our old European allies (France, Germany, and Great Britain) have socialistic democracies. The people heavily rely on the government for everything. In reality, the government has largely replaced religion in Western Europe. There is a cradle-to-grave social service policy that is about to break the back of these countries, especially France and Germany.

By and large, Western European nations, as well as Canada, think we Americans ought to be ashamed of ourselves for allowing our government to set us as a model for the rest of the world. After all, who are we, as an upstart, young pup of a country, to tell the world how it should live?

In fairness, Great Britain has begun the process of updating and streamlining their governmental social services, because the people just cannot be taxed any more than they are right now. They are a perfect example of what I call the *paradox of government.* If you give it all away in the good times, people will love it; but they won't let you take it away in the bad times. How out of sync the world is when people depend on the government to organize and rule their existence. People *are* the government. There is no power in the government without it being given to them by the people . . . who get it from God. Back to that pesky Declaration of Independence . . . .

It is hard for most Americans to understand, in view of everything our country has done for the various nations of the world, how these nations can look down on us, even hate us to certain degrees. Whether it was our reluctant takeover of the building of the Panama Canal or the recent outpouring of governmental and private help for the tsunami victims in the Pacific region, America has always been there to pick up the slack from the rest of the world. Faced with insurmountable odds, we usually do the right thing and win at what we set out to do.

Even the biggest "failure" of the twentieth century, the Vietnam conflict, was a political rather than a military failure. It was a lack of resolve by our political leaders to carry out the mission. The men and women who fought and died in that conflict did their job honorably and the politicians let them down.

So why do people who should know better—seemingly educated people who think they know what our country is—actually know so little about our country? Why do people fear the freedom our republic gives them? We saw unwavering support from the newly formed democratic republics in Eastern Europe. In the war on terror, these countries have given so much in contrast to what they have. I spent some time on panels defending the war effort and I was always amazed that Bulgaria and Albania and other countries that are new to freedom were made fun of, laughed at because they only sent a comparatively few soldiers to the fight. Their sacrifices mean as much to this conflict as ours do. They give all they have and I will always respect that.

Why do these small countries get it and some of our older European friends don't? The answer is simple: these new countries are closer to the time of their enslavement than their older neighbors on the continent are. We saw it again in the Ukraine during their recent elections. The people of the Ukraine who were new to freedom were not going to go back to Mother Russia. They were going to be the masters of their domain. The former government thought they could freeze them out, but they couldn't. Freedom in their sights gives people the power and strength to beat the odds. It was true when the United States first fought for its freedom and it's true today.

So far, I hope to have convinced you that America is not designed to make its decisions by raw popular opinion. As well, I hope to have convinced you that America is designed to make its decisions according to certain authoritative principles in the Declaration of Independence. And finally, I hope to have convinced you that America is in fact a self-governing republic, the authority of which enters our governmental system via the individual. In the next chapter we will consider the logical connections that meld our authoritative principles to our republican system of government.

Presidents as the Voice of the American Purpose

We dare not forget today that we are the heirs of that first revolution. Let the word go forth from this time and place, to friend and foe alike, that the torch has been passed to a new generation of Americans— born in this century, tempered by war, disciplined by a hard and bitter peace, proud of our ancient heritage—and unwilling to witness or permit the slow undoing of those human rights to which this Nation has always been committed, and to which we are committed today at home and around the world. Let every nation know, whether it wished us well or ill, that we shall pay any price, bear any burden, meet any hardship, support any friend, oppose any foe, in order to assure the survival and the success of liberty.
    —-John F. Kennedy, Inaugural Address, January 20, 1961

I am a fan of presidential speeches. My favorite is President Abraham Lincoln's second inaugural address. Almost every time I go to Washington, DC, I am sure to go by the Lincoln Memorial and read his remarkable address engraved there on the wall. It always brings me to tears. As a Southerner and as an American it conjures up images of a time when our nation might have been divided permanently. It is right and good that the Union was preserved. This great experiment had to be preserved; Lincoln knew it, and with a plurality of support he had to lead a nation through war and then had a vision of how to lead it through peace. His death led to the infighting among factions that tried to undo much of what we fought for to preserve this nation. Since 9/11, I have seen new meaning in the words. It is imperative that this war on terror is fought, won, and followed through to the end. So, yes, I cry at the base of the speech that Lincoln gave as his second inaugural address, but they are tears of thankfulness that I am an American and live in this great country.

Then I walk up the hill to the Vietnam Veterans Memorial and that also brings me to tears. The area on the mall that leads from the Lincoln Memorial, to the Korean War Memorial, and now to the World War II Memorial reminds us of the great sacrifice Americans have made to preserve this union. Additionally, these monuments serve as symbols to remind us all of the privilege and the costs of being an American.

In a discussion of the history that unites us as Americans, we need to look at important speeches in our history as a nation. One of the chief responsibilities of the president of the United States is to state our national purpose and the means by which it can be furthered. There are moments of presidential prose that take us back to our noble roots, that fill listeners with pride at our national accomplishments. But too often these speeches have been about what programs should be implemented or how taxes must be spent. There is so little that can inspire the patriotic heart in such an address.

The United States will not be acknowledged and respected by the rest of the world for our petty partisan fights over this or that governmental program. Our nation will not be remembered in history for the filibustered shutdown of senatorial processes. It will not be looked up to for the number of government handouts to lobbyists and special interest groups. America will only continue to be held up on the pedestal of world opinion for our vision, for the inspiration of our leadership, for the realized dream that hard work and seized opportunity can make the world a better place. Our greatest days are not made by bureaucrats. They are made by able leaders who embolden the American vision and who inspire the American people and the people of the world to live up to that vision.

America will be remembered for the battles she fought and the blood she shed for her independence and for the independence of others. After the world Economic Forum in Switzerland in January 2003, Colin Powell was confronted with the charge of an overuse of the "hard power" of military might rather than the "soft power" of diplomacy. Powell replied,

> We have gone forth from our shores repeatedly over the last hundred years and we've done this as recently as the last year in Afghanistan and put wonderful young men and women at risk, many of whom have lost their lives, and we have asked for nothing except enough ground to bury them in, and otherwise we have returned home to seek our own, you know, to seek our own lives in peace, to live our own lives in peace. But there comes a time when soft power or talking with evil will not work where, unfortunately, hard power is the only thing that works.

Words do matter. But what matters is that they are more than merely spoken, as Bill Clinton was masterful at doing. It also matters that words lead to honest action—that what is said is truly meant, as Ronald Reagan did and as George W. Bush has done. A perfect example we can consider is President Bush's second inaugural address.

Words That Inspire

The speeches of George W. Bush are messages of freedom. They appeal to the best in us. Some presidents have the gift of vision and are able to communicate that vision to the nation and the world. Many more do not. Lincoln, FDR, Kennedy, and Reagan had it. George W. Bush has it as well. A few people believe President Bush to be a failed communicator. I would argue that he is a clear communicator who simply may not have the charismatic delivery of Ronald Reagan. But people understand what he says and that he means what he says. In this, President Bush, like Reagan, trumps the empty rhetoric of an able orator like Bill Clinton every time.

On my first trip to New York after the terrorist attacks on America in 2001, I was in a cab with a driver who didn't like the president. He said, "Your Mr. Bush, at least when he says something you know that he means it." The most important way a president can establish credibility with the people is for his words to match his actions. When it counts, President Bush is there with the clear message that the job will get done.

When President Bush spoke to the nation at his second inaugural address, he was in the best position of his presidency. He had just been reelected as president with the first popular majority in fifteen years. This majority win gave him political capital to spend on the war on terror and on domestic policy. The economy was improving with remarkable job growth and an 8.6 percent increase in personal income for the previous year, according to the Department of Commerce. There had been a successful election in Afghanistan and was the promise of the first free elections in Iraq. With all of this recent success behind him, the president had much to be proud of as he delivered this address.

The Democrats, of course, are in the untenable position of having only negative responses. In America, negative messages don't sell. Unfortunately for them, the Democratic Party at this juncture appears to be simply a messenger of manufactured doom and gloom. They don't inspire the nation or even, in the notable case of former senator Zell Miller, many members of their own party. Winning a majority of the popular vote and the electoral college, George W. Bush had the most overwhelming election win in almost a generation; it cannot be denied that the American people have given the president a mandate to lead. And that he does, through word and deed.

When I listened to the speech given by President Bush for his second inauguration, I was reminded of some of the famous addresses given at times of great crises in our nation and the strong presidents who delivered these addresses. For Lincoln, it was saving the Union from rupture while directing the rightful end of slavery. For FDR, it was saving Europe from the totalitarian regimes of Nazism and Fascism while fighting the aftermaths of the Depression at home. For Kennedy (even though his time was short, he had a grasp of what was ahead), it was the fight against Communism abroad and for our own national civil rights at home.

As in those times, we are challenged today by the presence of extraordinary evil in parts of the world; it is evil that wants to seek us out and do us harm. For Bush, the challenge is the evil of terrorism—a difficult, if not impossible, enemy because it is not state sponsored and can change readily. But this enemy has to be fought.

I am sure there were those who thought the Confederacy would be impossible for Lincoln to defeat. There were surely those who believed the Great Depression would never end and that Germany and the Axis powers were too much for us in World War II. If the critics of America had their way, Communism would still be thriving in large parts of the world and Kennedy and Reagan would not have been successful in ending that tyranny. Those who wear the banner of naysayer are out in force every day.

This is why inspirational speeches by our leaders are important to the fabric of America. People are moved by leaders who have the ability to communicate their passion for America. Great leaders do not act alone. Rather they direct and motivate others to work with them for the betterment of our nation. A whole population of naysayers can work to deflate American pride, but it often only takes one able leader to inspire a generation to greatness.

Words That Strengthen

The strongest point about President Bush's second inaugural address is that he outlined and recommitted us to the ideals in our Declaration of Independence and the Constitution. As Newt Gingrich wrote in his book *Winning the Future,* "We have to go back to patriotic education. There is nothing wrong with focusing on the greatness of this country." The Declaration of Independence and the Constitution are about great ideas and so should be the cornerstone speeches of a presidency. President Bush's second inaugural address was about using the power of government to change government. It was a new way of looking at things and a new way of bringing the ideals of our founding fathers back into our daily consciousness.

The words of the oath of office that require a president to swear to uphold the Constitution of the United States of America reflect a deep commitment in the undertaking of the office. President Bush understands this level of commitment, as the first few paragraphs of his second inaugural address reflected when he said, "We celebrate the durable wisdom of our Constitution, and recall the deep commitments that unite our country. I am grateful for the honor of this hour, mindful of the consequential times in which we live, and determined to fulfill the oath that I have sworn and you have witnessed." By using the words, "deep commitment," the president referred to the indivisible nature of these United States of America.

President Lincoln also understood that nationhood cannot be withdrawn unless all contracting parties agree. This, together with the expressions of Article VI, Section VI of the Constitution which require the federal government to guarantee to the states a "republican form of government," was all Lincoln needed to justify his use of force against the rebelling southern states. President Kennedy said and recognized where the power came from in this country when he said, "In your hands, my fellow citizens, more than in mine, will rest the final success or failure of our course. Since this country was founded, each generation of Americans has been summoned to give testimony to its national loyalty. The graves of young Americans who answered the call to service surround the globe."

President Bush continued his inaugural address by saying, "At this second gathering, our duties are defined not by the words I use, but by the history we have seen together. For a half century, America defended our own freedom by standing watch on distant borders. After the shipwreck of communism came years of repose." September 11, 2001, was like many of the defining days of our republic. It is ironic the plotting for this day came during what we thought were "years of repose."

As a young woman, I shied away from using the words "evil" or "hate." They were too absolute for me. They indicated a loss of hope, and I never wanted to be without hope. But I had not been tested. September 11 changed all that for me and for everyone of character in this generation. We could no longer stand by and let evil work unhindered. We had to be involved.

I keep on my computer a picture of the side of a ship that was deployed to Afghanistan. It lists the events that went unanswered, from the bombing of the Marine barracks in Beirut to the attack on the *USS Cole*. The final entry is the terrorist attacks on America on September 11, 2001, which *have* been answered. The caption of the picture is "why we are here." Simply said and powerfully portrayed. Appeasement never works.

In his inaugural address, Bush showed that history is repeating itself—or at least its challenges. From the time of the Northwest Ordinance enacted in 1787 to the Dred Scott Decision of 1857, Congress's position on slavery changed from the hope of gradual elimination to the goal of a balance between the number of slave states and the number of free states. Lincoln understood that unless someone did something, the balance of power would tip toward tyranny and away from freedom as the number of slave states surpassed the number of free states. He sought to contain slavery, which was tolerated out of necessity but forbidden to proliferate.

Bush has taken the opportunity created by the events of 9/11 to seize the momentum and use that energy to force tyranny into a dark corner. Bush used Lincoln's example as a source of faith to know his goal is attainable. After all, Lincoln once did it in America.

There is a similarity in the language in the Kennedy inaugural address: "In the long history of the world, only a few generations have been granted the role of defending freedom in its hour of maximum danger. I do not shrink from the responsibility, I welcome it." President Kennedy was also a man who looked at America's challenges as opportunities to show the world what America was made of. President Bush believes as his visionary predecessors like Kennedy did. He knows what makes America great and what it takes to get Americans behind that ideal.

Words That Unite

In the second inaugural address, President Bush went on to say,

We have seen our vulnerability—and we have seen its deepest source. For as long as whole regions of the world simmer in resentment and tyranny—prone to ideologies that feed hatred and excuse murder—violence will gather, and multiply in destructive power, and cross the most defended borders, and raise a mortal threat. There is only one force of history that can break the reign of hatred and resentment, and expose the pretensions of tyrants, and reward the hopes of the decent and tolerant, and that is the force of human freedom.

Bush continues, as Lincoln and Kennedy did, to take our mission as Americans on a global scale, rather than a national one. Granted, during Lincoln's time he was talking about the areas of this country that "simmered in resentment." The idea that the newly formed Republican Party spoke out against slavery, a form of tyranny, and labeled it as wrong caused many Southerners to resent the new northern political movement. In their eyes, this new political party posed a threat to the Southern way of life.

Today, whole regions of the world resent America because when we speak or act out against tyranny, we threaten their way of life. Lincoln predicted in his "House Divided" speech that a crisis, no doubt a violent one, would gather and raise a "mortal threat" to the union. During that speech, Lincoln stated plainly that one or the other would prevail: "Either the opponents of slavery will arrest the further spread of it, and place it where the public mind shall rest in the belief that it is in the course of ultimate extinction; or its advocates will push it forward, till it shall become alike lawful in all the States, old as well as new—North as well as South."

During the mid-nineteenth century, Lincoln understood the importance of "tipping the balance of power" in America away from the forces of tyranny and toward those of freedom. As indicated by Condoleezza Rice's comments during her confirmation hearing as Secretary of State, Bush plainly understands the importance of accomplishing the same goal on a global scale. Both Bush and Lincoln indicated by their remarks an understanding that there is only one force in history that can eventually drive tyranny into extinction and that force is the universal urge for human freedom.

President Bush further makes the case for freedom and liberty, as in his own time President Lincoln did, by saying,

> We are led, by events and common sense, to one conclusion: The survival of liberty in our land increasingly depends on the success of liberty in other lands. The best hope for peace in our world is the expansion of freedom in all the world.

President Lincoln told mid-nineteenth-century Americans, "In giving freedom to the slave, we assure freedom to the free—honorable alike in what we give, and what we preserve. We shall nobly save, or meanly lose, the last best hope of earth." Similarly, President Kennedy said, "Let every nation know, whether it wished us well or ill, that we shall pay any price, bear any burden, meet any hardship, support any friend, oppose any foe, in order to assure the survival and the success of liberty. This much we pledge and more." (Sounds a bit like, "you are either with us or with the terrorists," doesn't it?) George W. Bush understands that by giving freedom to the slaves of other nations, we will be "honorable alike in what we give, and what we preserve." By doing so, Bush hopes to help "nobly save the last best hope of earth," that being America.

As in only a few times in history, America's vital interests and our deepest beliefs are now one. From the day of our founding, we have proclaimed that every man and woman on this earth has rights, dignity, and matchless value because they bear the image of the Maker of Heaven and Earth. Across the generations we have proclaimed the imperative of self-government, because no one is fit to be a master and no one deserves to be a slave. Advancing these ideals is the mission that created our nation. It is the honorable achievement of our fathers. Now it is the urgent requirement of our nation's security and the calling of our time.

Our vital interests being one with our deepest beliefs conjures images of both George Washington's farewell address, as well as Thomas Jefferson's first inaugural address. Our "vital interests" represented by the major political parties and those parties as "one with our deepest beliefs" indicate a desire for only one political party—an America united in spirit. That was Washington's dream for all future generations of Americans. It was Jefferson who said, "We are all Republicans; we are all Federalists." An America united in spirit was his vision as well.

Jefferson's Democratic-Republican Party almost pulled that off. For nearly twenty-eight years, America was really one political party. You may remember from high school American history the "era of good feelings." That was the middle portion of that twenty-eight-year epoch. The party of Jefferson finally broke into two halves during the election of 1828 when Andrew Jackson became the first to attempt to redefine the American form of government from a self-governing republic, run by the rule of principled law, to a democracy ruled by popular opinion. Attempts to do the same are still being made today.

Like our founding fathers, President Bush understands that God wants all individuals to be free. That is because only free people are able to do God's will. God's natural laws require that all people are equally free to pursue happiness. God's providence ensures that happiness naturally comes to those who do God's will. Because we are all created in God's image, God wants the best for us. After all, our happiness is God's happiness.

Inherent to this discussion is the idea that we are all "of God." Because we are "of God" we are all part of God. And because we are all part of God, we are all equal. And because we are all equal and "of God," no man "is fit to be a master, and no one deserves to be a slave." That is because to enslave a man is to enslave "part of God."

Words That Protect

Bush understands, to a certain degree, the authoritative nature of the American principles. According to Bush, "advancing these ideals is the *mission* that created our nation." The idea that the Declaration of Independence issues a "mission" to America implies that certain authority is dedicated to tackle that mission. In other words, America is "authorized" to pursue that mission. We are authorized by the one and only "author of liberty." But because over the years we have been perhaps lax in the execution of that mission, or perhaps because we have in certain ways even violated that mission in the eyes of God, it has now become "the urgent requirement of our nation's security, and the calling of our time." In the past, in order to maintain a critical balance of power in the world, America has violated that mission by choosing certain dictators and coddling them. We were engaging in a policy of "the enemy of my enemy is my friend" and it failed on September 11. We will not engage in that kind of foreign policy again. The Bush doctrine is that America will no longer coddle dictators. Either those nations are with us or against us. The leaders of those nations will have to decide their nations' courses and live with the consequences. It is because we have been attacked that this requirement has become "urgent."

In the second inaugural, in addressing freedom, President Bush said, "So it is the policy of the United States to seek and support the growth of democratic movements and institutions in every nation and culture, with the ultimate goal of ending tyranny in our world." Bush has pledged the full faith and support of American power to help free the world's slaves. This is a powerful statement, one that will either be looked back on as a hallmark declaration in the history of the world, proclaimed by a great visionary, or as an overly optimistic idealism uttered by a naïve but well-meaning footnote in history—a sort of "peace in our time" expression. I choose to be optimistic. Others will choose pessimism or cynicism. Bush agrees with me. (Note: When Bush speaks of "democratic" and "democracy," what he really means is "self-governing" and "self-government." Many people, meaning well, confuse those terms. We should not be confused; there is a difference when put into practice.)

In his second inaugural address, the president went on to say,

[Freedom] is not primarily the task of arms, though we will defend ourselves and our friends by force of arms when necessary. Freedom, by its nature, must be chosen, and defended by citizens, and sustained by the rule of law and the protection of minorities.

And when the soul of a nation finally speaks, the institutions that arise may reflect customs and traditions very different from our own. America will not impose our own style of government on the unwilling. Our goal instead is to help others find their own voice, attain their own freedom, and make their own way.

This is Bush's disclaimer. Even though we may not recognize freedom and self-government when put to use by other cultures does not mean it is not occurring. The proof will become apparent when peace abounds and those cultures no longer threaten their neighbors and our nation.

The president continued, "The great objective of ending tyranny is the concentrated work of generations. The difficulty of the task is no excuse for avoiding it. America's influence is not unlimited, but fortunately for the oppressed, America's influence is considerable, and we will use it confidently in freedom's cause." In this statement President Bush recognizes he will be out of office in four years. This is his charge of authority, a sort of "permission slip" if you will, for future presidents and representatives of the people to pursue these goals. As well, this statement is a chiding to those who might forego the responsibility. Furthermore, Bush is telling future leaders that although "Rome was not built in a day," Rome would not have been built at all without adequate effort. America will use our influence confidently because the cause of freedom is just. It is just because only free men are free to pursue God's will. The subjects of tyrants are not so free. Because God will provide for those who do His will, those who do His will can do so with confidence.

Bush shows his understanding of the magnitude and responsibility of the chief executive officer of this nation in making the statement, "My most solemn duty is to protect this nation and its people against further attacks and emerging threats. Some have unwisely chosen to test America's resolve, and have found it firm." He understands government's primary responsibility is securing God's endowment of rights to mankind. The first step toward fulfilling his job description is to protect the American people themselves against attacks and emerging threats. The idea that some have "tested" America's resolve echoes Lincoln's address at Gettysburg: "Now we are engaged in a great civil war, 'testing' whether this nation, or any nation so conceived and so dedicated, can long endure." These tests of resolve and endurance are all part of the great American Experiment. During the process of that experiment, America's resolve will be "tested" over and over. As during the Civil War, America's resolve to endure this test of fighting terrorism has been firm and has been clearly communicated by the words of the president.

President Bush continued,

> We will persistently clarify the choice before every ruler and every nation: The moral choice between oppression, which is always wrong, and freedom, which is eternally right. America will not pretend that jailed dissidents prefer their chains, or that women welcome humiliation and servitude, or that any human being aspires to live at the mercy of bullies.

The president uses the term "bullies," which indicates he understands that tyranny is universal. In another time, Lincoln understood that slavery was wrong. But he also understood he had limits on his authoritative power to do anything about it. He once said, "I am naturally antislavery. If slavery is not wrong, nothing is wrong. I cannot remember when I did not so think, and feel. And yet I have never understood that the Presidency conferred upon me an unrestricted right to act officially on this judgment and feeling." Although the limits to his authoritative power would not allow Lincoln to act on his feeling against slavery, he could use his position to constantly remind Americans that that institution is "always wrong." In much the same manner, Bush has chosen to clarify the issue for the world to consider with regard to self-government as the best antidote to terrorism.

There is a global appeal to liberty. President Bush articulated this notion in other speeches by saying "freedom is not America's gift to the world, but God's gift to humanity." God wants us to be free to perform His will on earth, and because doing God's will is the ultimate justifiable act, there can be no justice without freedom.

Intellectuals on the Left have questioned the global appeal of liberty—the fact of the matter is they believe some people are not able to govern themselves. I am sure the British in the time of the American Revolution believed the colonists could not govern themselves.

Americans, of all people, should never be surprised by the power of our ideals. Eventually, the call of freedom comes to every mind and every soul. We (the people of the planet) do not accept the existence of permanent tyranny because we do not accept the possibility of permanent slavery. Our great nation can do much to protect the cause of freedom around the world.

Words That Free

President Bush believes freedom is on the march. The power of our ideals when put to practice is multiplied by the favoring wind of divine providence. No earthly power can register against the ultimate universal power of the Creator. All human power is but a subset of the Creator's power. For this reason, human power can never rise above the power of the Creator. It is the American mission to use the wind of divine providence to free the world from tyranny. President Bush, as President Kennedy before him, stated in his second inaugural address that, "Today, America speaks anew to the peoples of the world: All who live in tyranny and hopelessness can know: the United States will not ignore your oppression, or excuse your oppressors. When you stand for your liberty, we will stand with you."

These words spring from the major premise of the Declaration of Independence, "All men are created equal." God's calling to America is to stand by those who are oppressed and to use the power He gives us so freedom may eventually command where tyranny once flourished. Democratic reformers facing repression, prison, or exile can know: America sees you for who you are—the future leaders of your free country. The rulers of outlaw regimes can know we still believe as Abraham Lincoln did: "Those who deny freedom to others deserve it not for themselves; and, under the rule of a just God, cannot long retain it."

The leaders of governments with long habits of control need to know that to serve your people you must learn to trust them. Start on this journey of progress and justice, and America will walk at your side. Trusting the people is necessary because no authority exists that does not first flow through the people. Therefore, any form of government that does not derive power from the people is a form of despotism. Despotism may be thought of as the "unauthoritative use of the power of government." In the mind of the Creator, for any nation to possess sovereignty, individuals must be allowed to express their authority by instituting a government. All other governmental forms are illegitimate, without authority, null and void examples of despotism.

> A few Americans have accepted the hardest duties in this cause—in the quiet work of intelligence and diplomacy—the idealistic work of helping raise up free governments—the dangerous and necessary work of fighting our enemies. Some have shown their devotion to our country in deaths that honored their whole lives—and we will always honor their names and their sacrifice.

With this statement, President Bush also echoed Lincoln's sentiments offered to the world at Gettysburg. As a basic responsibility of our citizenship, all Americans must give their undying respect to those who gave "their last full measure of devotion" to the cause of human freedom so that they "shall not have died in vain." The willingness of some to sacrifice their lives in order to perpetuate the freedom of others to do God's will is the ultimate evidence that humans are born with an innate understanding that "all men are created equal." In God's eyes, to give one's life in exchange for the freedom of others is an "equal" trade. Sometimes such a sacrifice for the sake of human liberty is necessary with the ultimate goal of extending freedom to all corners of the world. There is no greater debt Americans have than to those who make their life's work the defense of this republic. So Americans never forget that responsibility, we establish holidays and locations to honor those who sacrifice for our freedom. To sacrifice for the freedom of others is the ultimate exhibition of faith in the American principles. Such sacrifice must always be honored.

This great sacrifice was articulated by President Bush when he made the following connection:

> All Americans have witnessed this idealism, and some for the first time. I ask our youngest citizens to believe the evidence of your eyes. You have seen duty and allegiance in the determined faces of our soldiers. You have seen that life is fragile, and evil is real, and courage triumphs. Make the choice to serve in a cause larger than your wants, larger than yourself—and in your days you will add not just to the wealth of our country, but to its character.

Our generation was tested by 9/11 the same way our parents were challenged by the fight against Communism or Nazism. Bush understands that each generation has the responsibility to protect, defend, and extend human freedom in the world.

American presidents identify our pulse at the time and move us in the direction of those who carry such lofty ideals as "all men are created equal." These are very high standards and are difficult to implement. To violate those standards is to enable the enemies of free institutions the "plausibility to taunt us as hypocrites and causes the real friends of freedom to doubt our sincerity." The Abu Ghraib prison scandal is a good example of the results of not practicing what we preach. Bush of course points out why we must be steadfast in our principled existence. Ultimately, the goal is for those principles to spread the earth. When these assaults on our ideals happen within our responsibility, we must act quickly and definitively. Bush highlighted that by saying, "From the perspective of a single day, including this day of dedication, the issues and questions before our country are many. From the viewpoint of centuries, the questions that come to us are narrowed and few. Did our generation advance the cause of freedom? And did our character bring credit to that cause?"

The president continued,

These questions that judge us also unite us, because Americans of every party and background, Americans by choice and by birth, are bound to one another in the cause of freedom. We have known divisions, which must be healed to move forward in great purposes—and I will strive in good faith to heal them. Yet those divisions do not define America. We felt the unity and fellowship of our nation when freedom came under attack, and our response came like a single hand over a single heart. And we can feel that same unity and pride whenever America acts for good, and the victims of disaster are given hope, and the unjust encounter justice, and the captives are set free.

Americans are all united virtually 100 percent at the level of the most basic common denominators—our love of freedom and our fellow man. To some, freedom merely means security; to others, the freedom to accomplish great things; and still others, the freedom to simply wake up and do what they want to do each day. At the most basic level of commonality, freedom is a powerful need felt by all.

Bush concluded his second inaugural address with these words:

We go forward with complete confidence in the eventual triumph of freedom. Not because history runs on the wheels of inevitability; it is human choices that move events. Not because we consider ourselves a chosen nation; God moves and chooses as He wills. We have confidence because freedom is the permanent hope of mankind, the hunger in dark places, the longing of the soul. When our founders declared a new order of the ages; when soldiers died in wave upon wave for a union based on liberty; when citizens marched in peaceful outrage under the banner "Freedom Now"— they were acting on an ancient hope that is meant to be fulfilled. History has an ebb and flow of justice, but history also has a visible direction, set by liberty and the Author of Liberty.

President Kennedy said it like this,

Whether you are citizens of America or citizens of the world, ask of us the same high standards of strength and sacrifice which we ask of you. With a good conscience our only sure reward, with history the final judge of our deeds, let us go forth to lead the land we love, asking His blessing and His help, but knowing that here on earth God's work must truly be our own.

For America to continue to be protected, it must perform. It must perform by adhering to the American principles. "We go forward with complete confidence in the eventual triumph of freedom" because we have faith in those principles, faith born from more than two hundred years of results in the American experiment.

Even in the age of instant communication, the carefully prepared remarks of our leaders tell us the most about who we are. It has been the job of our leaders since the Declaration of Independence was first read in public and the Liberty Bell was sounded in celebration to the most recent speech given by a president on what America's responsibility is to itself and the world. At that first reading of the Declaration, a witness said about the ringing of the Liberty Bell, "It rang as if it meant something."

In our time, it means something still. America, in this young century, proclaims liberty throughout the world, and to all the inhabitants who want to stand for it. Renewed in our strength—tested, but not weary—we are ready for the greatest achievements in the history of freedom. The words of this president, like many other great presidents before him, inspire us as a people. They connect us to our past and point us toward a better future. They uphold our better values and strengthen our reserve against our weaknesses. That's what a leader with vision does through his words and his deeds. They unite where the negativity of naysayers might divide.

CHAPTER FOUR

Political Parties:
The Rise and Fall of Political Power

*The only Democrat who was successful in the 1990s was Bill Clinton.
We [Democrats] lost the House and Senate, governors' races and
mayors' races all over this country.*
> —Maynard Jackson, Former Mayor of Atlanta
> and Candidate for DNC Chairman, 2000

Party politics have always been dirty. It's simply the nature of the
beast. But there is a difference in the dirt these days. Much of this
difference can be attributed to the blur of the twenty-four-hour news
cycle. With the pressures of filling an entire news day and attracting
that all-important ad revenue, journalistic caution is often jettisoned
in the attempt to report first and fastest. Politicians are too ready to
access this instant communication with the public as well. Today,
before even attempting to talk to the White House or members of
the administration, members of Congress call press conferences and
complain directly to the news media. The twenty-four-hour news
cycle is a hungry beast, indiscriminately devouring careless, instant
information. However, because there is such a need to fill time, there
are more voices being heard, and I am one of those voices. I am
thankful for the opportunity, but because of the need to "feed the
beast," my responsibility to be right is even greater.

From the cab driver to the corporate executive, most Americans believe there is a problem with public debate in this country. Instead of our leaders sitting at the table and solving our problems face-to-face, they go to the microphones and hash out their difference in the press. We have seen this, for example, in the non-debate on Social Security reform in early 2005. No great changes in the history of this country happened that way.

Politicians and their parties have always been captivated by the want of power and the forward push of ideology. That hasn't changed. But in today's high-stakes, media-driven world, the political parties often make their cases to the TV cameras or the radio microphones rather than to the people. Their messages come fast and furious and their talking points, meant to appease the fragile sensibilities of target voting blocks, often obscure and hinder the true exchange of ideas. But how did we get to this point? And are parties really now much different in tone than they were in the past?

A Brief Tale of Early Party Politics

Even in our nation's earliest political elections, two political parties had overwhelming influence and politicked for control. The two contenders for president in the 1796 election were Vice President John Adams, a Federalist, and Secretary of State Thomas Jefferson, a Democrat-Republican (also notably called, at different times, Democrats, Republicans, and even popularly as Jeffersonians. Political parties were in flux in these days). These men were two titans of the Revolution. Neither of them campaigned publicly. They had surrogates very involved in the election, and it was a nasty fight. Jefferson was said to be lacking in religious faith and was too enamored with the French. Adams was attacked for being fond of the monarchy and for being aloof. Adams won the election with 71 votes to Jefferson's 68. At that time, each of the electors would vote for a candidate and the top vote-getter would be president, and the number two would be the vice president.

The election campaign of 1800 was a partial replay of the campaign of 1796, with the Democrat-Republicans opposing Federalist policies, but with one crucial, party-driven change. The Federalists attempted to mute the attacks of the Democrat-Republicans through the controversial Alien and Sedition Acts of 1798, which declared it a crime to make defamatory statements about the government or the president.

As a result of this legislation, twenty-five editors, most of Democrat-Republican newspapers, were arrested and their newspapers forced to shut down. One of the men arrested was Benjamin Franklin's grandson, Benjamin Franklin Bache, editor of the *Philadelphia Democrat-Republican Aurora,* charged with libeling President Adams. Bache's arrest erupted in a public outcry against all of the Alien and Sedition Acts. The constitutionality of these laws was questioned and public opposition to the acts was so great that they were in part responsible for the election of Thomas Jefferson, a Democrat-Republican, to the presidency in 1800. Once in office, Jefferson pardoned those convicted under the acts, and Congress restored all fines paid with interest.

Even without the Alien and Sedition Acts, John Adams faced substantial opposition within his own party for the presidency in 1800. As in today's political climate, the politicking for power was certainly not limited to struggles with opposing parties. Alexander Hamilton opposed Adams's reelection and led a failed scheme to have Charles Cotesworth Pickney, meant to serve as Adam's vice president, receive more electoral votes and thus become the president. But the defeat of the Federalists came when the New York legislature, dominated by supporters of Jefferson, provided the Democrat-Republican with twelve key electoral votes.

The Federalists' defeat, however, did not end the election of 1800. The Democrat-Republicans made the mistake of assigning the same number of electoral votes to both Thomas Jefferson and Aaron Burr. Thus no one had the majority of votes and the election was turned over to the House of Representatives. The House deliberated from February 11th to February 17th and voted 36 times. The Federalist congressmen had decided to support Burr, whom many felt was a lesser evil than the "dangerous" Jefferson. They would have won since they were the majority of the outgoing House. However, the Constitution called for the election of president by the House to be on a state-by-state basis. The Federalists simply could not carry enough states. On the 36th ballot, Thomas Jefferson was selected as our nation's third president, but the country had come very close to having Jefferson's own party-mate, Aaron Burr, instead.

The Dangers of the Two-Party System

The birth of the political parties in America came as much from how we elected presidents and vice presidents as ideology. For the office of president, the founders originally set up a system whereby individual candidates would run for this highest office and the two who received the most votes were named president and vice president, respectively. From our tale above, John Adams, elected in 1796 as our second president, was a Federalist, while his vice president, Thomas Jefferson, was a Democratic-Republican. Soon afterward evolved our present system of parties having a "ticket" of a presidential and vice presidential candidate running together. With this evolution came the birth of "party politics," a continuous power struggle within the individual political parties that has often done as much to dilute and endanger the ideals of the parties as it has to define and promote them.

The danger of political parties and the power to which they aspire has not changed much in our national history. The biggest risk the parties run is that to stay in power, they have to expand their beliefs to incorporate more people. The unfortunate result is that the more the parties expand their views to accommodate and capture votes, the less committed the parties become to the principles that got them elected and defined their political stands in the first place.

This dilution is particularly dangerous today because the laws in most states tend to protect the two dominant parties—Republican and Democrat—and prevent third parties from rising naturally into power as they have for most of our history. It is relatively easy for almost anyone to get their names on the ballots of statewide congressional races, as well as national presidential races. One of the problems with the Florida presidential fiasco in the 2000 election was that there were ten candidates running for president. Eight of those candidates didn't have a prayer of being elected, but there they were crowding and confusing the ballot anyway.

However, in races where a third party candidate could actually stand a chance of winning, like local and state offices, it is almost impossible to get on the ballot. On these levels, the power of individual personalities and the presentation of ideals important to the people could affect the election of politicians outside the dominant parties. But the election commissions instead often protect Republicans and Democrats from the rise of other parties. It is highly irregular for a new party to emerge today as they did in the early days of the republic. Democrats and Republicans control the elections commissions in states and determine how candidates can achieve ballot access.

In most states the party machine wants to protect its power so it limits access to smaller, newer parties. The two major parties don't mind giving ballot access to offices a third party candidate has no chance of winning, but they don't want to allow ballot access on local, winnable offices. It is time for additional political parties to emerge, but the party structure won't allow it.

Since I believe the United States is a center-right country ideologically, I also believe the make-up of our national political parties would look much different if political parties were left to their own devices to bring in converts rather than being tied to the local and state strictures of the traditional two-party system. If local and state politics was left to its own devices to allow the growth of other parties to national prominence, I believe the Republican Party would be the most prominent nationally, by far. It would encapsulate the vast majority of like-valued voters in this country. The few in the Far Left would control the Democratic Party or abandon it for the Green Party. The few in the Far Right would fill out the Libertarian and Constitution parties.

The Era of Ideas Is Back

The conventional wisdom is that elections and political parties are nastier than they used to be. One look at our earliest presidential elections proves this not to be true. Politics is and always will be nasty and prone to corruption. The combination of money and power is an unparalleled aphrodisiac. This is probably why the founders wanted citizen legislators who went back to their home states after a time of service. Statesmen are not prone to corruption, but it is hard to find a politician who has not been tempted. The only way to combat the corruption is to lead with vision and then leave the office before power has a chance to corrupt.

Of course, politicians want to win and they wouldn't pursue the kind of campaigning and party politics practiced today if they didn't have egos to match their desire to win. The problem is principles. When candidates and political parties lose sight of their principles, they tend to lose elections. As corny as it sounds, political parties win elections when they do as they promise, or when they are perceived to have done as they promised.

The best political public relations coup in history is the perception that the Civil Rights Act and the Voting Rights Act were products of the Democratic Party. This was truly an American victory. Americans had already decided that Civil Rights was an issue they had to reconcile, so many of their elected leaders followed suit. At the signing of the Civil Rights Act of 1965, President Lyndon Johnson specifically thanked Republicans for the bipartisan effort that was more cultural and regional than based in party politics. Since then, however, Democrats have taken credit and Republicans have been afraid to stand up for what they did. Democrats, to their credit, were able to convince the American people that their party was the party of opportunity for minorities. The problem is that it was all style and no substance.

Democrats have talked a good line on racial equality but in actuality haven't done anything about it. The Democratic leadership has been beholden to the traditional African-American organizations like the NAACP. That has gotten them out of the mainstream of African-American life, especially with the growing African-American middle- and upper-income earners. The Democratic Party stopped going to the people and expected the vote to be delivered by these organizations on the strength of their overstated Civil Rights record. But that tide is changing. The group vote is largely over. The respect for individuals is what will keep people voting for a party, despite the workings of party-bound political action committees.

The irony is that in the future Republicans will need to guard against the same tent-widening failures of the Democratic Party while wooing minority voters. In the last election, 42 percent of the Latino vote went to George Bush. But that vote did not come from group endorsements; it came from the Bush campaign's brilliant outreach into all communities with door-to-door volunteers and the president taking his message to the community. The danger is that powerful Latino groups lobby out of Washington, DC, and they want to speak for Latinos just as the Rainbow Coalition or the NAACP presumes to speak for all African Americans. We don't yet know who the Jesse Jacksons or Kweisi Mfumes of the Latino voting populations will be or if there will be one at all. But all politicians in general and Republicans in particular must be wary of falling into groupthink regarding the Latino vote. Individuals within a group have individual needs, so we cannot expect a group to vote one way.

In the last two election cycles, traditional groups didn't vote in "traditional" ways, and Democratic strategists worry that 30 percent of the African-American vote is up for grabs. If that is true, the Democratic Party is finished in America. It stands to reason that as African Americans get farther from the days of segregation, they will vote along socioeconomic lines rather than color lines. Again, we are moving away from groupthink and toward individual freedom, which is bad for the Democrats.

Right now, conservatives and the Republican Party in particular are attracting lower- and middle-income voters at record levels because conservatives represent opportunity and values. Minorities should come to the Republican Party because it is the party of economic opportunity for the individual as well as the party of faith-based moral values. Rather than rely on tradition and old styles, Republicans choose to judge others by their character and qualifications. This must be communicated to minority voters truthfully and directly, without assuming their votes will come automatically. If we learned anything from the elections of 2004 and the 1.5 million volunteers mobilized on the Republican side through direct media, it's that the era of groupthink is over and the era of ideas is back.

Recently Craig Shirley wrote a book detailing Ronald Reagan's failed 1976 presidential bid for the Republican nomination. In *Reagan's Revolution: The Untold Campaign that Started It All,* we see Reagan's unparalleled ability to run on principle and vision, to rely on strong ideas apart from the constraints of party politics, and to bounce back from personal defeat. This works for those driven by principle, as was Reagan and as is George W. Bush. These men are not just politicians; they had successes and failures outside of politics. Their successes or failures as human beings were not defined by winning or losing an election. Had either man been unsuccessful in reaching the White House, he would have gone on to do other great and noble things. In addition, election losses would not have changed their principles.

We like to think our problems and the way we handle them are unusual to our time and place. But people react to the acquisition of power the same way whether they are in the eighteenth century or the twenty-first century. The issues of today are not much different than the issues of yesterday. They are based on unchangeable core values. The situations these values are applied to are different, but the judgment used to decide on the course of action doesn't change. The core values and steadied principles of the founders should be what we look for in the leaders of today.

Look back on the presidents of the twentieth century and whether their successful election to the United States presidency was a watershed mark for their party that took it in a new direction or just another win for a philosophy. I would argue that in every case in the twentieth century, the election of a president hinged on how the party solidified its identity around a consistent, singular vision. There were only two times in the twentieth century when Republicans had to "go into the wilderness" and regroup: once after the defeat of Herbert Hoover and again after the defeat of Barry Goldwater. But after each of those defeats, Republicans came back stronger and put together unifying positions for this party.

The greatest danger for any party is that in its quest to stay in power, it compromises its values. The Democrats are where they are today because in the 1960s and 1970s, they opened their political tent to every Far Left fringe group in the country, from feminists to gays and lesbians to radical environmentalists. Little by little the middle class that had identified with the Democratic Party felt more and more out of place. And as the Democrats are beginning to learn from the shift of public sentiment toward the Republicans, the power of a strong, sensible idea will trump the power of empty, open rhetoric every time. The era of ideas is back, indeed.

Give 'Em Zell

It is clear Democrats have lost their vision in the post-Clinton era. The late Maynard Jackson was right on target when he said Bill Clinton was the only Democrat to have real success in the 1990s. If you looked at mayoral races, gubernatorial contests, and congressional elections, Democrats have lost ground consistently throughout the 1990s and into the 2000s. Jackson, a successful African-American politician from Georgia who had put together a grass-roots coalition to run the city of Atlanta as the first black mayor of that city, ran for the chairmanship of the Democratic National Committee after the 2000 election. He was right in his assessment of the state of the Democratic Party and was thanked by being dismissed and relegated to a position of anonymity in the party. Terry McAuliffe was chosen again to lead the party into great fundraising years and more defeat at the polls.

Terry McAuliffe presided over a close race in 2000. In 2002, he presided over something that hadn't happened in seventy years—an incumbent president picking up seats in the Congress at midterm. In 2004, he continued the pattern. In the two other times in our history with as close of an election as 2002 was, the incumbent was not reelected. Bush was reelected and picked up more seats in the House of Representatives and the Senate—another milestone for the president's party and another historic loss for the Democrats. Amazingly enough, instead of leaving the party in disgrace, McAuliffe left the

DNC portrayed as a winner. He raised more money than any DNC chairman in history, but he lost every major contest he presided over.

The Democratic Party continues to lose ground. There has been a ray of hope here and there—a couple of mayoral races have gone to the Democrats and a couple of governor's mansions now have Democrats in them again—but by and large, Democrats have lost ground since 2000.

In his bestselling grievance against the Democratic Party of his birth, *A National Party No More*, Zell Miller laid the foundation for getting back to the Scoop Jackson, John Kennedy, and Harry Truman days of the party. In response to this and to the former senator's latest book, *A Deficit of Decency*, Democrats who have never won an election say Zell Miller isn't a Democrat. Try telling that to the man who won nine statewide elections for a party he loved and who, just three years ago, was sought by Democrats in Georgia and across the nation to cut campaign commercials for them. Zell Miller not a real Democrat? Please. A real Democrat (or Republican, for that matter) is someone who can win elections for their party and gain ground, not lose it.

Democrats have now suffered major losses in 1994, 2000, 2002, and 2004. The issues were the same in each of those defeats. Democrats thought they knew better than the voters did, and the voters told them who is boss. Bill Clinton, Joe Lieberman, and Dick Gephardt understood that, and they stood firm with the values most Americans believe Democrats should have. Look where they are today. Bill Clinton, while successful, is a dream that will never be as big in history as while were living it. He was the epitome of the "me generation" he said he loathed. He was the gluttony of the '80s manifested in the '90s. Joe Lieberman and Dick Gephardt are out of power and probably will never run for president again. But they stood for something, and I believe history will be kind to them in the end. Their party will benefit from modeling their values.

As far as political parties go, Democrats should choose someone who represents mainstream values. An interesting contrast is that President Clinton was able to put a voice to these values and successfully appeal to the middle of America, while Joe Lieberman and Dick

Gephardt have shown these values over time (but the party did not relate to them in the 2004 primaries). Miller put the strongest voice to the problems of the Democratic Party, but he has been treated as an outcast.

It is ironic that the Democrats of today are turning to Howard Dean. While donations increased substantially right after his nomination, money was not the problem in the 2002 or 2004 elections. Chairman McAuliffe broke fundraising records over and over. John Kerry even had money left over at the end of the campaign. Common sense would suggest that someone from a winning endeavor would be made chairman. Maybe they would reach back to someone who had actually orchestrated a winning campaign or won a presidential primary outside of his own home state. Instead, they chose Howard Dean, the former governor of Vermont and loser of the Democratic nomination for president in 2004.

To put it in perspective, Vermont is smaller in population than most congressional districts. In the 100 fastest-growing counties in America with populations over 10,000, the Democrats lost 97 and none of them was in Vermont. This is not to knock small places; small towns and rural America are the backbone of this country and they are the strongholds of the Republican Party.

Dr. Dean is out of step with what it takes to lead the Democratic Party. It really isn't entirely his fault; he had help from the media frenzy around his campaign and its meteoric demise. The media made us think he was a winner before the first vote was cast. He raised a great deal of money from nontraditional sources that gave over and over again. But his only win at the polls was the Vermont primary, and he spent all the money he had. That is one thing John Kerry didn't do. He was never really the frontrunner once the first vote was cast.

Democrats are at odds about what to do. Is the message right, but average Americans just can't understand the nuances, as Nancy Pelosi and John Kerry believe? Or could it be that the message is right and it wasn't communicated clearly, as President Clinton has suggested? The divide was clear in the comments of this most successful Democratic president since FDR, who said, "There were too many voters who didn't really know why we were Democrats except we were against the president's policies." But then John Kerry said, "This great party of ours doesn't need a makeover."

It is clear the party still doesn't know what to do with winning Democrats like Zell Miller. In his bestselling books and speeches across this country, Senator Miller has talked about many of these issues. In discussions with Southern delegates to the election of Howard Dean, I've found they still believe they have been left out in the cold, like they are the outcasts in the Democratic Party. It seems that trying to win in quickly growing states might be a good idea, but not one Democrats want to pursue.

It is unfair to say Howard Dean had no Southern strategy in his run for the presidency. He made more of an effort in the campaign than either of the nominees for president or vice president did. He actually asked Democratic leaders in the South for their votes in the primary. He visited President Jimmy Carter at church and showed his clear understanding of the divide in the party when he said, "White folks in the South who drive pickup trucks with Confederate flag decals on the back ought to be voting with us, and not (Republicans), because their kids don't have health insurance either, and their kids need better schools too." He'll surely woo the red states with that attitude. For the party of the little guy, it seems Dr. Dean needs to get out more.

Zell Miller, even after his infamous speech in New York during the RNC—and possibly because of it—ought to be *embraced*, not shunned, by the Democratic Party. They all ought to be making a pilgrimage to Young Harris, Georgia, to ask his advice. Miller was overwhelmingly elected in a state that has gone from 4 million residents to 10 million residents in the last 40 years. This state has faced its race problems head on and, while not perfect, Atlanta has more wealth in the hands of African Americans than any city in the world.

Zell Miller has been a tax-cutting, government-streamlining, education-supporting champion throughout his career, and when Republicans were winning all over Georgia, so was the ultimate Democrat, Zell Miller. You would think Democrats would look to those leaders of their own party who have been successful in such circumstances. It doesn't mean anything to be a Democrat who wins in San Francisco, Boston, or Chicago. It takes conviction of principle to win as a Democrat when all around you the other party is gaining.

In the next five years, our Republican-dominated government will revamp Social Security, simplify (and hopefully replace) the current tax code, and deal with health care delivery in this country, all while working to defeat terrorism around the world. To get any one of these accomplished would solidify Republican Party power for a generation. If the Republicans are successful, will they know what to do with it or will they be victims of their own success? If they take the example of the Democratic Party in the last decade to heart, it may be a long time before we see anyone but a Republican in control of our government.

The American Compass

We have the moral constitution as American people to find our way in this world. We are not nearly as divided on the major issues of our time as some forces might want us to believe. Mainstream America is right-of-center. It was during the drafting of the Declaration of Independence and it remains so today. As a people we hold a moral compass on most issues that steers us surely and clearly into the future.

Recently, I had the opportunity to talk to with comedian Tom Rhodes, who spent four years working throughout Europe. I asked him what Europeans disliked most about Americans. He said it was our optimistic nature—that, no matter what, we look at things in a positive light and that our sheer will to succeed usually leads us to victory. Much of Europe hates that about America, but the description is true nonetheless.

True Americans will " let every nation know, whether it wishes us well or ill, that we shall pay any price, bear any burden, meet any hardship, support any friend, oppose any foe, in order to assure the survival and the success of liberty." These words spoken by John F. Kennedy in his Inaugural Address in 1961 epitomize what America stands for and how our nation will be remembered through the course of history. This is the American compass.

CHAPTER FIVE

Health Care in America:
The Role of Personal Responsibility

When people find out that managed care is really managed cost, they won't want it anymore.

—P. K. Dixon, MD

Access to good health care is what everyone wants. But at what cost? And how should we define good health care? When government manages health care, the costs go up. The best (but not the only) example of this was in 1965, when the original *thirty-year projection* for Medicare was $6 billion. By 1967, the $6 billion was spent and the first Medicare price freeze went into place.

In 1967, Congress knew the formula for Medicare was not working. It would have been easier to fix it then when the provision was not expected and when relatively few people relied on the system. But instead, here we are in 2005 still putting Band-Aids on a Medicare system that represents the largest unfunded mandate in the history of the world at about $27 trillion over the next fifty years.

There are two things at play here. First, government miscalculates the future costs of just about everything. One of the few things former Secretary of the Treasury Paul O'Neill said that was right on the money was when he was questioned about the wild fluctuations in the deficit and surplus projections. After pointing out that this was nothing new, he said we should deal with the here and now. To the point, if we deal with today's problems today then we won't have to deal with them tomorrow. If we do that, when the unexpected problems come up—and they always do—resources can be allocated to the new problem. The problem with health care delivery and payment today is that we knew there was a problem with delivery issues in the sixties and have just rolled those problems over since then. Problems avoided do not get better, they just get worse.

Second, when people think someone else is paying for something and the access is unlimited, then they will overuse it. In the first two years of Medicare, more money was spent than was projected for the first thirty years of the Medicare system. In 1967, we knew there was a problem; the concept of "it's already paid for" brought many more people to the doctor. Now this has probably led to the dramatic increase in life expectancy among seniors, but as this model was expanded to all age groups, we are paying a very high price for the convenience of not having to collect directly from our insurance providers. Remember when your mom or dad used to sit at the table, matching up the form to the receipt before mailing in the claim form? That was when the insurance companies were accountable to the customers because they had already paid the doctor for services rendered, and individual customers were going to make that insurance company accountable. They followed up until they got an answer.

With all the hand-wringing about the 45,000,000 or more uninsured in this country, the fact is that most of the uninsured in America are employed and have health-care coverage offered at work, but choose not to participate either because they can't afford it or they don't want to pay for it. It has been estimated by the Kaiser Family Foundation Commission on Medicaid and the Uninsured (July 2004) that, of the uninsured, about nine million are employed with health insurance offered to them. If you include their dependents as uninsured, they account for two-thirds to three-fourths of the uninsured in America. There are people who can afford health care but won't buy it at any price. Their priorities are out of sync, and they think luxuries are necessities. Anyone with an iPod, a cell phone, and cable television—but no health insurance—has grossly misplaced priorities.

My friend Dave Ramsey, host of one of the most popular financial advice radio shows in America, has talked often about the "four walls" you must have for some amount of safety and stability in your life. They are food, shelter, clothing, and transportation. He recently added health insurance to this list.

My husband is a primary care physician. Most of the uninsured people he sees are young and employed and have the option to buy health insurance. When they tell him they can't afford it, he asks them if they can afford an illness that could cost $10,000 or more to treat. Health insurance has to be one of the necessities in every budget. It should come before expensive cell phones, cable television, Internet access, or a new car. Not only does having health insurance allow better and more consistent care, but it's part of being a responsible member of society. Responsible citizens should be unwilling to take from the taxpayers what they can provide for themselves.

People are not being denied care in this country. The question is, at what cost? Our overall quality of health care has been affected in recent years by the various costs associated with many issues, but the three most important are the lack of personal responsibility among many of our taxpayers, the attempt to make everything a Medicare model, and the drain on the system caused by illegal immigration.

Personal Responsibility

Our genetic make-up is something we have no control over, but most health problems today are related to lifestyle choices. We can complain about the environment or the "toxins in our pocketbook," but the fact remains that if we were to eat right, exercise regularly, drink alcohol only in moderation, and not smoke, we could rid our society of many of its chronic and life-threatening health problems and reduce health costs dramatically. Think of all the money and resources that would be freed up to deal with genetic health problems if we took responsibility and lived healthier. The medical resources spent treating us for the bad things we do to ourselves are beyond measure. My husband Lin says only half-jokingly that if people quit smoking and drinking and started eating right, he would have nothing to do all day. But instead of doing what we should do, we want to walk out of the doctor's office with a magic pill and the permission to do whatever we want. This is not to say we all have to be bodybuilders, but if we expect the government to "catch us when we fall," then we have to take some responsibility.

We want to blame industry—the tobacco industry, the fast food industry, the beer and liquor industries—for our own bad choices. I have had a problem with my weight all of my life. I could blame it on heredity or on the fast food nation—and maybe some of that is fair—but mostly I gain weight because I choose to take in more calories than I expend. As much as I hate it, to keep my weight under control, I have to eat right and exercise. The older I get, the more I have to keep watch on these things. It's my responsibility to myself and to my family to do so.

I laughed out loud at the August 2004 *Newsweek* cover story on fat and weight loss. The article went into great detail on all the options out there. The most interesting thing is that it seems every time someone tries to attack fat with chemicals, the fat proves smarter than the chemicals. After a while, the fat wins. After all of the discussion of new ways to lose weight with this or that magic pill or procedure, the final paragraph of the cover story basically says the only sure way to lose weight is to eat less and exercise more. How boring! And how commonsense!

As the mother of four children who have gone to public school, I believe one of the problems in schools is the limited activity the children have during the day. Even though physical education classes and recess are being cut to make more time for test preparation, physical education and intramural sports need to be expanded in schools, with an emphasis on active play. If we increase the activity level in school, children will be healthier, and test scores will rise. Another problem in public schools is the children's access to junk food. I applaud Gov. Arnold Schwarzenegger and other activists for their efforts to remove vending machines from schools. It is again up to adults to lead by example. At school just as at home, we must turn off the TV, get outside, and limit snacks.

In America today, the tobacco industry is being targeted by people who want to blame it for the health problems related to smoking. Newsflash: Cigarettes can cause health problems like lung cancer. If you began smoking before the Surgeon General's warning, then I will give you a pass on this, if you are still alive. But if you began smoking after the Surgeon General's warnings started showing up on the sides of every pack of cigarettes and on every print ad, there is one word for you—*dumb*.

I have never owned a pack of cigarettes, but I smoked them occasionally for about fifteen years. I was dumb for fifteen years. I will admit I loved smoking. It relaxed me. But about ten years ago, I couldn't stand them anymore. Maybe it was because of my children. I really didn't want them to smoke. But honestly, cigarettes just began to make me sick, so I quit for good. Believe it or not, there are still women who smoke because they are afraid they will gain weight. Again, there isn't a better word for it—*dumb*.

I will never forget the commercial that ran after the film and stage actor Yul Brynner died of lung cancer. I saw that handsome face with that thick accent saying, "If you are seeing this, then I have died of lung cancer. If you smoke, quit. If you don't, don't start." It was as simple as that. My father was eighty-one when he died of lung cancer. The doctor said his heart was strong, but his lungs were shot. My dad smoked until he was seventy-seven. He was diagnosed with lung cancer in May 1991 and died in August 1991. I am thankful he only felt sick for about ten days before he died. But I was cheated by cigarettes, and so was my family. I was pregnant with my daughter when he died; one of the last things he said to me was how beautiful I looked at six months pregnant. He never saw my daughter and that has caused me and her pain. The cigarettes weren't worth it. Throughout his life, my dad had a couple of broken bones and a broken back while he was in the army. All of the other hospitalizations and illnesses were related to smoking.

Think of the resources that could be spent on other things if people didn't smoke. I am not an advocate of making smoking illegal.

I am an advocate of people being responsible for their own behavior. As Yul Brenner said, "If you smoke, quit. If you don't smoke, don't start." These are words to live by.

It is unfair to the taxpayer for anyone to abuse his or her body over a lifetime and then expect us to pay for it. I think that even applies to Medicare patients. We ought to keep our promises, but we need to begin today by saying if a terminal health problem is caused by individual irresponsibility, we will make the patient comfortable, but we won't spend anything to prolong that patient's life.

That makes you pretty mad at me doesn't it? It should make you mad. No one should plan their life so that others have to pay for it. People who are on a taxpayer-funded health-care plans should get benefits for changing an unhealthy lifestyle and saving money, as if living longer and healthier wasn't benefit enough. We must all regain a sense of personal responsibility. If we eat right, exercise, don't smoke, and don't drink in excess, we will probably have a long and healthy life.

Let's be clear: I don't think the government should make us start doing the right thing for our health. We should decide that for ourselves. Anyone who decides to keep overeating, smoking, and drinking shouldn't expect the taxpayer to foot the bill for inevitable chronic health problems. We have to make a stand on this today for future generations.

Medicare

David Walker is the comptroller general of the United States of America. He heads up the Government Accountability Office (GAO) and crunches numbers all day long while worrying about this country's ability to meet its obligations. He worries particularly about Medicare. About two years ago I attended a speech he gave in Gainesville. He laid out a case about our nation's fiscal health that would scare the pants off you. While the annual budget deficit, the tax code, and Social Security are all concerns, the biggest problem facing us in Walker's estimation is meeting Medicare responsibilities. The potential costs of Medicare as baby boomers enter the Medicare system boggle the mind. The trustees of Medicare and Social Security typically estimate costs based on a seventy-five-year cost outlook. In 2004, the trustees dramatically departed from past practice and included an estimate of the cost of Medicare and Social Security based on an "infinite horizon" instead of the usual seventy-five-year cost outlook. The trustees found that, eventually, the total gap between the cost of promised benefits for the two programs and the revenues to pay for them will be close to $50 trillion. Based on the traditional projections, the long-term gap between cost and revenues would be $18 trillion over seventy-five years. In fairness, these estimates don't take into account cost savings measures taking effect in 2006 or the implementation of the prescription drug plan. Most experts agree these changes won't make things better and might make them worse over the long term. Medicare and Social Security have to be changed totally to work in the future.

The Office of Medicare and Medicaid Services is talking about spending your money on things that should never be paid for by taxpayer dollars. Medicare and Medicaid recipients have to be mindful that government has no money of its own and any benefits are paid for by the taxpayer. In the case of Medicaid, all the money is collected from the general public and dispersed to those who are in need. Medicare is paid for by withholding from payroll in the form of FICA taxes throughout someone's working life. Not more than 45 percent of it budget can come from the general budget and the balance is from premiums Medicare recipients pay for physician coverage. But it is all *taxpayer* money.

One of the big drawbacks of Medicare is that it had been a catastrophic model until some changes were made in the last decade. It was originally designed to handle hospitalization and catastrophic care. At its inception, most people only had one hospitalization after sixty-five, and it resulted in their death. The life expectancy was in the 60s, so most people wouldn't make it to Medicare age—or to Social Security for that matter. And if they did, the remainder of their life was short. Medicare was designed as a catastrophic health-care plan without a preventative care component. Changes have been made to move toward preventative care, but it's not moving fast enough.

Since then, progress has been made, but the bureaucracy is just not catching up with the advances in medicine. By nature, government programs are difficult to change. In 1967, when Medicare met its cost projection for the first thirty years, Congress knew it had a problem. In 1967, Medicare wasn't an entitlement and could have been fixed. From a medical standpoint, it is much cheaper to catch a problem earlier and manage it with medicine than to have several major operations. Right now we are in the transition period, so we are paying for both. But if we stick to the reforms to Medicare, we should see improvement in the system. Right now and until we see the benefits from long-term management of chronic illnesses, we are paying for preventative care as well as catastrophic care. As the population ages, this is going to be the biggest financial and social problem we face in our society.

Illegal Immigration

We are the most generous country in the world, but even the most generous people in the world have a limit, and the American taxpayer has reached its limit on the costs of illegal immigration. The two issues that are most affected are education and health care. We'll discuss this in greater detail elsewhere in this book, but let's consider it here in the context of our national health-care crisis.

The federal government is not doing its job in regard to illegal immigration, and our states and cities are drowning because of the federal government's abdication of its duties outlined by the Constitution. This is particularly true with rising health-care costs for the treatment of illegal immigrants who cannot or will not pay for their own medical care. This issue must be addressed, or local hospitals and emergency care facilities (who do not turn people away) will be hurt the most.

No one advocates that sick people should be turned out on the street. Illegal immigrants cannot receive Medicaid and are expected to pay for all medical services. But there is a burdensome loophole for emergency care in regard to illegal immigrants in most states (including my home state of Georgia) called Emergency Medicaid.

For example, most pregnancies are not emergencies and don't require transportation by ambulance. However, in Atlanta there are facilities called Clinica De La Mama that provide prenatal care to immigrant women (both documented and undocumented) for a flat fee. When it is time for the birth, the clinic arranges for an ambulance to pick up the woman at the clinic and take her to the hospital, creating an artificial emergency status for the delivery and burdening the taxpayer with the cost. This must stop. Americans are generous people, but there has to be fairness. These costs will continue to be incurred until the federal government enforces the law and secures the border. I did not choose this example to pick on mothers who are illegal immigrants. The most complicated thing about immigration is the mixed status family. Often one parent is here legally; another is here illegally, and some of the children are citizens while others are not. We are not going to deny care to a person in need, but if the Federal government did its job enforcing the border, we would see this problem correct itself over time.

We need to insist that our government either enforce the immigration laws that are on the books or come up with a system that shares the burden. It is difficult to talk about immigration, especially illegal immigration, without looking at its effect on education and health care. Americans are not going to turn away sick people, and we are not going to let children wander about uneducated. In our desire to please everyone, we are failing. The biggest factor in controlling this entire situation is a tightly controlled border and deporting people when our law requires it. Recently Rep. Charlie Norwood and the House Caucus on Immigration have put forth the best analysis of immigration and potential solutions that I have seen. This comphrensive study on immigration is worth our govenment's consideration.

Aging and the End of Life

With all the praising the Left does of the single-payer system (nationalized medicine), the dirty little secret is that many procedures in such a system are limited by age. In other words, if you are over a certain age you don't get a heart bypass or a knee replacement. We were used to saying "do everything you can" to make our loved one's life better. The cost wasn't important. But then we lost track of what things actually cost, and now we, the consumers, have no idea of the real cost of any medical procedure. It is easy to say "do everything you can" if you are not going to have to write a check to pay for it. In socialized medicine it is common for people to be told they are too old for a procedure. America is not ready for that.

All of us, not just the aged, also need to talk about what we want done at the end of our lives. Over half of the health costs of a lifetime are spent in the last month of life and these expenditures don't usually change the outcome. We don't want to limit care, but it is important for people to know how far they want to go once they know they are not going to recover.

I dedicated this book to my dear friend Patti Stephenson. I visited her the night before she died of breast cancer in October of 2004. She knew she would die, and she knew she wanted to be comfortable, to have her friends and family around her, and to have fluids. There probably could have been some heroic procedures done to extend her life a week or two, a month or two more. But at what cost to her and what cost to her family? I know the instinct is to do everything possible, but there also has to be a clear line that you know is the end. The most important thing that Patti did, as difficult as it was, was to communicate to her family what she wanted at the end of her life. We all need to do this.

Hospice is one of the unsung heroes of this movement. None of us wants to talk about death, but we should research our local hospice, talk to our doctors, and make these decisions for ourselves. We should talk to our families and, if possible, handwrite a letter outlining what we want to do at the end of our life. Our families will benefit, and we will too. If we are going to be responsible about health care, we have to consider these things. This spring we all lived through the death of Terri Schiavo, but out of Terri's life and death, I hope people will talk to their loved ones about their wishes for the end of life. If our life ends at thirty-five, sixty-five, or ninety-five, we owe it to the people we love to be at peace in death.

If all this discussion about death seems a little unseemly in a chapter about controlling health care costs, it isn't. Half of health care costs for your entire life are spent in the last month of your life. They are usually spent with no chance of changing the outcome. Every person is different, but it's important that before extraordinary measures are taken, we know what the person wants. If we do not know, we have to err on the side of life, which is why we must have the conversation, follow it up with the proper documents, and update the information as we age and as our desires change.

CHAPTER SIX

The Abortion Debate

No woman wants to have an abortion.
Teresa Heinz Kerry, *Time Magazine*, June 2004

One of the truest statements ever spoken—no woman wants to have an abortion. For over thirty years we have been debating the wrong side of this issue. President Bush said it best when he entered office. He said he had no intention of trying to overturn *Roe v. Wade* because changing the laws won't change the rate of abortion in this country. The hearts and minds of the American people have to be changed—and they are changing. On moral issues we have to be reeducated.

One of the major mistakes of the Republican Revolution of 1994 was that conservatives, social and otherwise, thought the country rejected liberalism and embraced conservatism. Rush Limbaugh has made this point repeatedly since then. The truth is that Americans were unhappy with the very liberal leaning of the first years of the Clinton administration and wanted to move the country back to the Right. While the country is center-right, many Americans still have to be convinced that conservatism is the best way to go. The hardliners on both ends of the spectrum will say these folks don't stand for anything. I would disagree; these voters are the non-party-line voters who will be influenced by policy stances and personality.

Conservatives need to continue educating. Offsetting the message the liberal media perpetuates of conservatives as Bible-toting, right-wing, pro-life nuts takes a great deal of work and commitment to ideals. The impression is that we are out of the mainstream, but the 2004 election proved we're not. President Bush understands that, and his message resonates with the American people because he is one of us.

On the issue of abortion, as with many conservative issues, the country is moving in the right direction. Those on the Left have said that abortions have increased during the Bush years. The fact is that some states have seen a rise in abortions, but overall various studies show us that the rate of abortion is declining about 1 percent a year under the current administration. It is not enough and doesn't change the fact that about 98 percent of abortions are done for convenience, not for necessity.

As a young adult, I bought into the liberal mantra about a woman's right to choose although I still believed in my heart that abortion was wrong. But I didn't want to seem narrow-minded or uptight, so I kept my mouth shut. Liberals want us to believe that having a clear view of right and wrong is rigid or short-sighted, that, to quote Obi-Wan Kenobi in George Lucas's latest *Star Wars* movie, "only a Sith speaks in absolutes." Apparently even a Jedi Master can be blinded by the force of a liberal Hollywood screenwriter.

Of course, there are areas of gray in life where judgment and discernment come into play, and that is where we take responsibility for our actions. The gray areas in life are why we need a moral foundation. The black and white issues are easy to decide; it's the shades of gray where we have to weigh the options and sometime decide between two difficult solutions. For example, when a pregnancy is unplanned, there was already a decision to have unprotected sexual intercourse. The next decision is what to do from there. This is where judgment comes into play. A moral compass kicks in, and there is a right and wrong answer—not just a right and wrong answer for you.

Remember the *Seinfeld* episode about homosexuality? Throughout the show, anytime the issue of homosexuality came up, the response would be, "Not that there's anything wrong with that!"

We have created a generation of people who don't want to offend anybody. We have to relearn in this country that it is okay to say something is wrong and still be compassionate about it. Having a traditional view of the world isn't intolerant. It's okay to say we are concerned about the way a person is living his or her life. In 1984, it was revealed that one of my co-workers, Bob, had AIDS. That day we went to lunch and talked about it. I said, "You knew this was out there; how could you have let this happen?" He said, "I didn't think it would happen to me." So many people go through life thinking, "It won't happen to me." Bob passed away four years later. At the time, four years was a long time to live after an AIDS diagnosis. He spent his last years mending fences with his family and taking care of other AIDS patients. In 1984, people didn't want to deal with people with AIDS. Bob did things no one else would do, and I believe God blessed him with a little more time because he was caring for the least of us.

On abortion, I tempered my position and consoled myself with the idea that I would never have an abortion, so I was okay. I bought into the idea that I shouldn't infringe on someone else's choice. Is that a nothing position or what? Just out of college, I had a friend at work who discovered she was pregnant. Her boyfriend had gone to law school. She didn't tell him she was pregnant because she knew he would quit school to come home and marry her because it was the "right thing to do." So she had an abortion. I will always regret that I didn't counsel this friend to tell her boyfriend and to have the baby. I will always regret that I didn't tell her there is nothing wrong with a man who wants to "do the right thing" and that a child didn't have to mean the end of either of their dreams.

Some Americans have been brainwashed by the left wing of the feminist movement into thinking that if we are enlightened, we should feel that abortion is okay, that our lives come first. The key word is *feel*. We don't want to make anyone feel bad about anything they've done. We don't want to expect anything from anyone that might lead to them calling us "right-wing nuts" or "moralists." But the feminist movement was and is perfectly fine with millions of women knowing that they made a horrible mistake in aborting their children. Having a clear sense of right and wrong was too simplistic and wasn't nuanced enough for the liberal feminists.

But this attitude misses the point. The reason abortion is wrong is that to kill a potential human life—a human embryo—a baby —because you made the choice to have unprotected sex is irresponsible. Ending a pregnancy because it's not a good time is wrong and irresponsible.

I know the liberals are screaming right now, "What about the victims of rape? What about the victims of incest?" These are legitimate questions. If we are talking about abortions that are a result of rape or incest, or that endanger the life of the mother, then we are talking about 2 percent of abortions. If irresponsible people will stop the abortions of convenience, *then* we can debate the few that remain. Anyone adult enough to enter into a sexual relationship should be adult enough to handle the consequences. The responsible thing to do is to have the baby and either raise the child or give the child up for adoption.

My friend J. C. Watts told me once that one of the big mistakes of the Republican Party is that it made single parents feel as if their families are not real or legitimate. He is right. I am not saying that single parents cannot do a good job. There may be circumstances where the mother can't or shouldn't marry the father of the baby. In that case, she will need a lot of help from her support systems. I have a friend who has raised three children without a stable father in the home. She has brothers and makes sure that her children have great men in their lives. Her children are all fine, taxpaying members of society, but it took hard work and sacrifice on her part to get them to that point.

Adoption is the second casualty of the abortion debate. Florida governor Jeb Bush recently suggested that counselors employed by the state should be able to discuss adoption, along with abortion, as an option for teenagers who find themselves with an unplanned pregnancy. Certainly the Left in this country will cry foul, presenting anything other than the choice of abortion as interference with a woman's body.

So what made me change my mind on abortion? When I was pregnant with my first child, I had a sonogram. When I saw the fuzzy outline of the fetus and the bright, beating heart, I knew I had been wrong about abortion and I quietly thanked God for never having to make that choice for medical or other reasons. I do believe abortion is wrong, but it should not be outlawed. It is a medical care issue, and if a woman needs to have an abortion, I would never want her to have substandard medical care. But I have never met a woman who was happy she had an abortion. Even if it was to save her own life, there is an ongoing sadness that is difficult to resolve. So I changed my point of view, but I realize there is common ground on both sides of this issue.

Most women, more than 70 percent according to many recent studies, won't even consider an abortion or adoption, but because we have taken this debate out of the doctor's office and into the courts, what do you think the outcome will be if a woman goes to an abortion clinic? She won't be counseled about adoption, that's for sure. Doctors should have the ability to counsel women on single parenthood, adoption, and abortion. But we also need to tell the truth about the long-term health risks and emotional trauma of abortion as part of that counsel. We should celebrate mothers who do what is right for their children, even when it's inconvenient for them. It's hard to be pregnant, and it's got to be even harder for a woman to give up for adoption a child she carried for nine months. But after talking to women who have had abortions, it is a lie to claim an abortion is easier. It might be quicker, but it leaves scars much greater than the choice of adoption might leave.

Let's set aside the labels of *pro-choice* or *pro-life* and look at the attitudes of most Americans, according to many recent studies. Sixty percent of the people believe abortion-on-demand is wrong. If I get more specific, the numbers get more dramatic. More than 80 percent of people believe abortion as a method of birth control is wrong and that only in cases of rape, incest, and danger to the life of the mother should there be exceptions. Almost all people believe the procedure called partial-birth abortion is wrong. While it is not an accepted practice you will find in any medical textbook, we know it is performed rarely in the US and, until recently, was performed most frequently in China. China recently had to admit the wholesale abortion of girls from their society had a detrimental effect that will take decades to rectify (*Wall Street Journal*, August 2004). How long will it take to heal the wounds of two generations of abortion-on-demand?

Statistics show that most people consider themselves to be pro-life, even if they do not use that label. In fact, right-to-life groups acknowledge the Left has done a good job in demonizing the term "pro-life." People in general are favorably disposed to the tenets of the pro-life movement, but if you ask individuals if they are pro-life, they may not use that label. Interestingly, people in the business of spreading the pro-life message have said their biggest surge in new membership came a year or so ago during the GE advertising campaign for their new sonogram machine, which shows an incredibly realistic image of a baby in the womb. When people saw the clarity of the facial features of the baby in the commercial, many of them called to join their local pro-life organization.

A poll conducted by *USA Today*/CNN/Gallup in 2003, as well as Gallup polls dating back to 1975, have shown the link between the attitudes of most Americans and the pro-life movement. The 2003 poll showed that 27 percent of Americans think abortion should be *legal* under any circumstances, while 16 percent say abortions should be *illegal* in all circumstances. It also showed that 55 percent said that abortion should be legal in cases of rape, incest, and danger to the life of the mother. Since those three exceptions account for less than 3 percent of the abortions in America each year, then more than 70 percent of Americans oppose 97 percent of all abortions. Americans agree on abortion in overwhelming numbers. The abortion-on-demand people are in the minority in this country.

Anyone watching the news or listening to the liberal fact-spinners might think this country was split 50-50 on this issue, but it is not. One of the largest groups changing their views on abortion is college-age women. More than 60 percent of that group now opposes abortion. Since they are the group of women most likely to have an abortion, the pro-choice "movement" knows if they lose this group, then the movement is all but dead. These are the mothers of tomorrow, and they shape the country's views on this issue.

The impressions given by the mainstream media are wrong on a number of other attitudes on abortion that are shown in the 2003 *USA Today* /CNN /Gallup poll and have been supported by numerous polls from other sources. The opposition to partial-birth abortion has grown from 55 percent to 61 percent, and the support has dropped from 40 percent to 34 percent. Seventy percent of Americans consider a politician's position on abortion when they decide how to vote.

Since *Roe v. Wade*, we have had a continual chipping away at the value of life in this country. We have murdered more than forty million babies in this country since this Supreme Court atrocity of *Roe v. Wade* was decided. The Terri Schiavo case highlighted the lack of respect for life that *Roe v. Wade* began. If you believe the statistics that only 2-3 percent of abortions are because of rape, incest or danger to the life of the mother, then close to 39.5 million of these abortions were performed because "it just wasn't a good time" to have a baby. Plenty of families would be happy to adopt these infants. We must restore the value of life in this country.

I want people to realize they have a choice whether or not to engage in unprotected sex. If that choice results in a pregnancy, then these same people need to realize there are many other options out there to keep that bad choice from turning into a worse one. I want women to get all the information they need to make a decision they can carry with them for the rest of their lives, because they will. We have to get back to a culture that values life at all stages, from conception through death. After all, doesn't this country that proclaims to value "liberty" and the "pursuit of happiness" also claim to value "life," first and foremost?

Justice Stephen Breyer likes to use foreign law in deciding cases on the Supreme Court when it suits him. Justice Antonin Scalia recently challenged that notion in several different venues. Basically, Scalia says you can have any law you want as long as you can convince enough of your fellow Americans that it's a good idea. He also pointed out that if we wanted to be in the mainstream on abortion, then we are only one of six countries in the world that allows abortion-on-demand. If Justice Breyer thinks we are out of the mainstream on death sentences for juveniles, then why doesn't he believe we are out of the mainstream on killing babies through abortion? I know this is tough language. I have always been reluctant to use the phrase "kill babies" when talking about abortion. I didn't think it helped the debate, but this language must be used. The value of life in this society must be elevated. President Bush discussed this culture of life in his speech to the nation on stem cell research in August 2001:

> My position on these issues is shaped by deeply held beliefs. I'm a strong supporter of science and technology and believe they have the potential for incredible good—to improve lives, to save life, to conquer disease. Research offers hope that millions of our loved ones may be cured of a disease and rid of their suffering. I have friends whose children suffer from juvenile diabetes. Nancy Reagan has written me about President Reagan's struggle with Alzheimer's. My own family has confronted the tragedy of childhood leukemia. And, like all Americans, I have great hope for cures. I also believe human life is a sacred gift from our Creator. I worry about a culture that devalues life, and believe as your President I have an important obligation to foster and encourage respect for life in America and throughout the world. And while we're all hopeful about the potential of this research, no one can be certain that the science will live up to the hope it has generated.

Many people don't know or remember that President Bush's sister, Robin, died of leukemia at four-years-old and how that tragic event shaped his life. Barbara Bush, his mother, spoke about it in her autobiography (if you haven't read *Barbara Bush: A Memoir*, you should). The Bush family understands medical research and the need for it, but they also understand that the foundation of our society is the value of life.

We are a nation that values life; there is no way around it. We should err on the side of protecting life. We are a pro-life nation. Live with it.

CHAPTER SEVEN

Race and Gender in America

*I've done the best I can to lead my life. I suppose I could have stayed
home and baked cookies and had teas.*

—Hillary Clinton, 1992

First of all, I have to thank Hillary Clinton. It was because of her and
the statement above that I called in to my first radio talk show.
Believe me, as hard as it is to juggle work outside the home and
family schedules, there is nothing harder than working full-time
inside the home. Hillary Clinton is a victim of the feminist movement that claimed that being an accomplished woman meant acting
just like a man. In the 1980s, many women even tried to dress like
men. But "equal opportunity" does not mean being equal in every
respect. Real women get that.

The stereotype that Hillary Clinton talked about during her husband's initial run for the presidency is indicative of the way leftists
think about women in this country. They are the ones who want to
separate us. It shows small-mindedness which people like Hillary
Clinton make a career of claiming to be against. Women in the real
world know that it's much more complicated than that. Many myths
in our nation grew out of the women's movement, and the same
could be said of the Civil Rights movement. But the people who live
and work every day in America know what the truth is on these two
most volatile issues of our time—race and gender.

Race in America

One of the greatest public relations coups in history is the idea that Democrats are responsible for the Civil Rights legislation successes or the 1960s. The truth can be found in the passage of the Voting Rights Act of 1965 and the Civil Rights Act of 1964, which were two of the truly bipartisan successes of our republic.

The United States Senate is the key to passing any comprehensive piece of legislation like this. By observing today's obstructionist Senate, much like the Senate of the 1930s–1960s, you can imagine what it was like trying to get Civil Rights legislation passed. Southern Democrats were hanging on to the past. Today's Senate Democrats are blocking legislation that will take this country into its next phase. The buzzword of that era was "states' rights." It was important to the founders that the central government did not have too much power over the states. That is why, until the passing of the 17th Amendment, senators were appointed by the state legislatures and governors in order to make the senators accountable to the states. Until the 17th Amendment, the states were the first priority of the Senate. Since then, the popular election of senators puts the states in line with everybody else, essentially just another special interest group with a cause to lobby. The Senate has become an obstruction-ist body because its members are owned and operated by special interest group lobbyists instead of the states they are supposed to rep-resent. Another unfortunate casualty of history is the belief that any time states' rights are used to oppose or defend a piece of legislation, then states' rights proponents are labeled " old-time segregationists" or "homophobic religious puritans." Nothing could be further from the truth. Today's contest is more likely to describe a person who wants to return to the meaning of the republic created by our Constitution.

When President Johnson signed the Civil Rights Act of 1965, he specifically thanked Republicans because twenty-two Southern, Democratic senators voted against the bill. He was careful in his wording by saying,

That law [the Civil Rights Act] is the product of months of the
most careful debate and discussion. It was proposed more than one
year ago by our late and beloved President John F. Kennedy. It
received the bipartisan support of more than two-thirds of the
members of both the House and the Senate. An overwhelming
majority of Republicans as well as Democrats voted for it.

Since the Democratic senators and representatives from the South
voted against the act, it truly took a bipartisan effort to the pass the
Civil Rights legislation. Isn't it ironic that it was the Democrats, who
today sell themselves as the party for minorities, who passed Jim
Crow laws, fought desegregation, and controlled governments in
cities and throughout the South?

My colleagues on the Left would say that all the segregationist
Democrats are now Republicans. But those numbers don't add up.
The fact is the majority of men who controlled the segregationist
South at the time have been dead for years, in most cases long before
the Republican revolution began. Republicans have been browbeaten
into feeling responsible for the problems of race in the country when
the fact is that Republicans have been responsible for putting people
of color in more positions of real power than Democrats ever have.

After the 2000 elections, Democrats had the chance not only to
show the increasingly Republican South that they were not ignoring
them, but also to put a young African American in the minority
leader's position in the House of Representatives. Instead they chose
Nancy Pelosi, a woman from the most out-of-the-mainstream district
in the country, to lead them. In 2000, two African-American stars,
Congressman Harold Ford Jr. and Maynard Jackson, the former
mayor of Atlanta, were brushed aside when Democrats desperately
needed to reach out to the increasingly Republican South and West.

For decades, Democrats have expected lock-step support from
the Congressional Black Caucus, but they never rewarded that support with leadership positions. Democrat leadership thought the
Congress wasn't ready for African Americans in leadership positions.
When J. C. Watts joined the House as a Republican, he was put in a

leadership position by his second term. Those same Democrats accused him as being a token to hide from the general public the truth that the Republicans didn't really believe in equality. But you can't continue to discount black conservatives in prominent places in the Republican power structure.

The only way to have power is for the political parties to have to fight for your vote. In November 6, 2000, Rep. John Lewis was on *The Martha Zoller Show*. I asked him if it served the purposes of progress in the African-American community to vote overwhelmingly for one party. He said that even though he was a partisan and wanted Democrats to win, it wasn't helpful for any party to know they were going to get virtually the entire African-American vote. Essentially he was saying that politicians should feel as if they must prove to every group that their vote is deserved.

According to Ashley Bell, the former African-American head of the College Democrats, African-American men are not predisposed to voting for Democrats anymore. Under his leadership, College Democrats increased membership for the first time in years. Republican politicians cannot discount the votes of people of color, either. However, the temptation is to adjust the message for minorities. That is not necessary, though. One of the messages of the Republican Party is colorblind opportunity. The party is about opportunity and optimism, faith and family. Republicans have the best record on opportunity for all people and, if judged on actions of the parties, not just words, the center-right coalition has the advantage with minorities in the future.

In the last few generations we have tried hard to right the wrongs of oppression and prejudice, and we should be proud of that. In our zeal to right the injustices of the past, we have gone too far the other direction and created new stereotypes through lowered expectations. To assume people of certain ethnicities will perform in certain ways or need certain help to succeed is to expect less from them. President Bush calls this "the soft bigotry of low expectations." It is not as overt as the "colored only" sign over the water fountain, but it is just as devastating.

Henry Louis Gates of Harvard University began the discussion again with his book *America: Behind the Color Line*, which argues that while government has a role to play in making sure things are equal and the playing field is level, it is also true the African-American community needs to lift up students who do well. Gates insists communities must emphasize excellence and instill high expectations in their children.

Perhaps the largest boost to this idea came from an unusual source—comedian and actor Bill Cosby. If you know anything about Bill Cosby, you know he stands for educational excellence. He stressed that to his own children and continues to do so now throughout the African-American community. He is a regular speaker at college and university graduations, and the message is always the same —expect nothing less than excellence.

Expectations are not about color, gender, circumstance, power, or money. They are what family, friends, church members, and neighbors believe you can achieve. As a country we need to get back to individuals being involved with and responsible to each other. Dealing with someone who will be disappointed in you is much harder than dealing with a government employee who has seen and heard it all before. Help is best given in families, neighborhoods, and religious circles.

Gender in America

Many of the arguments that apply to issues of race in this country also apply to gender issues. This is the century of the woman, and the movers and shakers of this century will be influenced by the women and the men who have supported them. Since 2000, there have been 25,000,000 women freed in Afghanistan and Iraq, not to become American women, but to become what they want to be. Girls are beginning to have an awakening throughout the world in countries that historically looked at women as second-class citizens.

George Washington knew the value of women and foresaw their growing power when he said, "Now would I rob the fairer sex of their share of glory of revolution so honorable to human nature? I think you ladies are in the number of the best patriots America can boast." Abigail Adams, one of the first American feminists, reminded her husband, John Adams, and Thomas Jefferson in their writing of the Declaration of Independence not to forget the "fairer sex" in the discussion of who was created equal. Abigail Adams had one of those relationships with her husband that most women wish they had. Through their letters it was clear they respected and loved each other and had a clear balance of power in their relationship. She was his equal in every way.

Throughout most of our history, the contributions of women have gone unmatched in the development of the American economy, especially in the development of the middle class. Women worked on the family farm, clerked in the general store, took in sewing, and did other jobs to help feed their families, in addition to the full-time job of raising the children. Women have always been able to keep many plates spinning at once. But as more women have entered the workforce with its demands on time away from home, their ability to juggle career and family has diminished.

In the 1930s, movies gave the impression of American extravagance through Ginger Rogers and Fred Astaire and the happy endings of Shirley Temple. When our men returned from World War II in the late 1940s, our world changed dramatically. Americans began to get their views of themselves from a new home reality—television. In post-World War II America, it was the little screen that gave us the image of perfect family life in *Father Knows Best, I Love Lucy, Make Room for Daddy,* and *Leave It to Beaver.* The new American image was of beautiful wives with perfect hair, well-behaved children, and pristine houses. Many women thought they had to live up to that two-dimensional picture of the idyllic family life.

The approaching radical feminism of the late 1960s and 1970s changed that image for many women. Many felt pressure to compete with men, to prove themselves equal in every way. They sought forms of liberation from the classroom to the boardroom to the bedroom. But the real struggle over women's rights was not between women and men, but rather between women and other women. An old saying goes "women don't dress for men; they dress for other women." Women are the hardest on each other about the choices they make. The biggest feud is between those few leftist, intellectually elitist, self-proclaimed feminist women and the majority of mainstream women who populate this country.

A poster girl of the former is Maureen Dowd of *The New York Times*. She writes caustic pieces about how men will never understand her, not because she is doing anything to repel them, but because they are not smart enough to understand her. She also has concluded that men don't want smart women. The truth is, they want smart women who will listen and be their helpmates.

Dowd is a fine writer, but she doesn't represent the views of the majority. Women come in all shapes and sizes with a variety of different needs and abilities. Yet for all that variety, women provide the solid and immovable foundation of this society that makes America what it is. Women don't have to say they are intellectuals to actually *be* intellectuals. Yes, even those of us who spend our days with our children making mac-and-cheese, coloring, and driving from dance classes to swim lessons can be considered intellectual women.

Much more so than the liberal talking head Maureen Dowd, our nation has a powerful example of the recent success of both women and African Americans at the highest level. Her name is Condoleezza Rice. She served in George W. Bush's first administration as national security advisor. In his second term, he elevated her to the position of secretary of state, succeeding Colin Powell. Holding this position quite possibly makes her the most powerful woman in the United States and arguably in the world. She is the second woman to be this close in the line of succession to the president in our history.

Her story is the story of many women and African Americans of the last fifty years. She has a story to which all women can relate. I love that she breaks all the stereotypes: she is feminine, intellectual, involved in the arts, and her dream is to become the commissioner of the NFL. She not only rose above the glass ceiling, she shattered it and will continue to do so. It does appear that her success has come at a cost, however. She is unmarried and has no children. She is a part of the first generation of feminists who believed things had to be compromised in order to achieve what she has. Compromise may not always be required, but having a husband and a family makes a career such as hers much more difficult.

The major message for women in today's American society is that they don't have to choose one life over another. They can have it all, just *not at the same time*. Women still are the primary caregivers on several levels, and most of us want to be. Making the society and our own expectations flexible will make the caregiving easier.

Lawrence Summers, the embattled president of Harvard University and former member of the Clinton administration, took heat when he commented in an academic setting that one of the reasons there are fewer women in the highest levels of math and science is that women frequently take critical time away from their professions in order to raise their families. Summers is right; there is a definite swing back to slowing down careers and taking family time. The fact is that most women don't resent the time they take to raise their families. Many don't mind that they may spend a few years moving a little slower for the benefit of their families. Few of us ever went to our deathbeds saying, "I wish I worked more," but many of us wish we had spent more time with our families. There is a finite time in which we can raise our families, but we can always work. When I speak to women's groups and especially college groups, I tell women to finish their educations. Then when they decide to marry or not, to have children or not, they have all the options at their disposal to make the most of their decision.

When I married in 1990, I became the instant mother of three young boys. I never in a million years thought I would want to stay home with my children or anybody's children, but after a couple of nannies, I realized that someone had to be there with them and I happily made that choice. The next year I had my daughter and that made four, and the next few years were filled with children. When my daughter went to school, I was offered an opportunity to do a little radio. I had a journalism degree from the University of Georgia, so I had the tools and I could go back to work on my own terms. I had an arrangement with the owner of the station; I won't ask for money if you don't ask for time. As long as the quality of *The Martha*

Zoller Show was superior, then we were all happy, but this arrangement gave me the power go to school for lunch if I needed to
without feeling guilty. I realize I had an incredibly supportive boss
and staff (more than once, Amy Harrison, one of our sales people,
picked up one of my children from school) and a supportive husband
who allowed me to afford that arrangement.

I recently gave the commencement address at Brenau Academy, a
girls' prep school in Gainesville. After the commencement was over, a
friend of mine, Dr. Mike Maloney, said, "You made being a woman
sound so good, you made me want to be one." Ah, if only he could.
Feminism in America has been a wonderful thing. It has opened up
opportunities for women our foremothers could have never
imagined.

I am a feminist in that I believe women should have equal opportunity to do what they are able to do. Women have options . . . I
might argue that they often now have *more* options and opportunities than men do. Women can enter and exit the workforce and
adjust their schedules without the kind of scrutiny men experience.
But the secret to true feminism at the beginning of this new century
is to recognize that equality is not only about money and opportunity. Feminism is not about a woman being the same as a man, but
about a woman being able to be fully woman. It is about making the
right choices for yourself, your children, and your family—whatever
those choices are—without feeling the pressures to spin all the plates
all the time. American women have come through the feminist
movement and they heard its true message. We are almost there.

Keeping the Whole Family Strong

Over the last few generations, women have been competing with
men in what was once seen as only a man's world. But the fact is that
while women are gaining rights and opportunities, men are doing
worse. There is a disconnect going on in our society. Roughly 20 percent more women than men go to college. The numbers are even
more dramatic in the African-American community. Half of the students enrolled in professional degree programs are women. Perhaps

there is a thing as too much progress, too much equality. When does equality for one become suppression of another?

We have spent so much time looking at the development of women and minorities that social scientists have only recently started looking at how boys are doing. Traditionally, boys test higher on the SAT, but fewer boys than girls go on to college. There is a higher dropout rate among boys, and if they do drop out, they are far more likely to end up in the juvenile justice system. Boyhood is endangered in this country and, rightfully, First Lady Laura Bush is taking on this issue in her husband's second term.

Boys are also diagnosed more often as having attention deficit/hyperactivity disorder, reading disorders, conduct disorder, autism, and stuttering according to *The International Journal of Men's Health*. Boys may be at greater risk for physical injuries that result in permanent altering of life opportunities because they believe they are tougher and healthier than they really are. They don't go to the doctor as often, and males usually have their diseases diagnosed in later stages than do women.

Issues with the roles of mothers and fathers still compound this problem. Women are more likely than men to have had someone talk to them about what it means to be a parent. I don't blame the schools or society for this; I blame the parents. Being a parent is a life-altering and enriching experiment; it is the most important job any of us will have. But we toss our families and our responsibilities aside as if starting over is the best thing to do. The National Marriage Project found that if we behave like adults and stay together in a marriage without abuse, addiction, or adultery, our children will succeed at higher rates as adults themselves. So the family is a key factor.

In this country there are equal opportunities, but the choices we make still affect those around us, including our children. In the wreckage of the sexual revolution, where feminism was hijacked by promiscuity and a culture of drugs, the divorce rates in this country skyrocketed to the detriment of the American family and, ultimately, our moral fiber. But the divorce rates are going down, and people, even veterans of the sexual revolution, are regaining a sense of decency as they rediscover the bonds of common values that unite our country and make us strong. The American compass continues to point us forward, straight and true.

CHAPTER EIGHT

Immigration

Either enforce the immigration laws or change them. The wink and a nod policy of today will not work.
—Congressman Nathan Deal (R-GA)

By nature of the title of this chapter, some ground rules have to be set. There is no doubt this country is a nation of immigrants. The majority of Americans who are concerned about immigration reform are not opposed to legal immigration. Most people who are concerned about this issue are not racists or bigots. Rather, they want the federal government to take responsibility for their role in this problem, to secure the border by requiring legal entry to and exit from this country, and to aid in ensuring that taxpayer-funded programs do not go to fund illegal immigration. The federal government must acknowledge and accept that their lack of diligence on this issue has cost taxpayers billions of dollars in health care delivery and public education costs.

Few issueshave been as discussed as much as immigration reform on local talk radio stations around the country. No issue is more tied to our national security discussions than immigration. The 9/11 hijackers used our immigration enforcement system, or lack of it, to plan and implement the attacks on America. This is one of the issues clearly defined in the Constitution as the responsibility of the federal government. The issue becomes disconnected because the federal government has the responsibility to secure the borders and determine immigration parameters, but they do not incur the state and local costs of education and health care associated with illegal immigration. The federal government does not understand the magnitude of this problem. But tax dollars are tax dollars whether they are paid on the federal, state, or local level, and taxpayers are paying for this mistake.

While I credit the Bush administration for raising the issue of immigration reform, they have not been diligent on illegal immigration. In fact, there has been a "wink and a nod" policy at the federal level by both parties for a generation. Republicans are keenly aware of their need to do better with minority voters while meeting the needs of the business community by not impeding cheap labor. Democrats want to maintain their foothold with minority voters. These are the dirty little secrets both parties won't admit, so the subject has not been discussed, and the number of illegal immigrants continues to grow. Even though the President did not say he wanted to grant amnesty to illegal immigrants when he introduced his proposal in January 2004, that is what the immigrant community heard, so the levels of illegal immigration have actually increased. The thought process has been, "If I get in, I won't have to leave," and up until now that has been a pretty good bet.

Advocates of loosened immigration policies say that immigrants come because employers want to hire workers for jobs Americans won't do. The other part of it is that welfare programs, which by law should not be given to illegal immigrants, are continually and rapidly depleted of funds because the government has tied its own hands regarding verification of the legal status of immigrants. Millions of tax dollars a year are spent to house, feed, clothe, educate, and care for illegal immigrants. Our message might as well be, "Cross our borders in the dead of night and board the gravy train of American generosity!" The fact is that our country rewards people for entering illegally.

My grandmother, Anna Martha Dolge, immigrated to the United States in 1903. She left and entered the United States twice before she was a citizen, and I can go to the Ellis Island website and pull up the ships registries for both of those trips. One of the ships she was on was the *Amerika*. I can read the handwritten questions she was asked and the answers she gave about entering the country. They asked if she was an anarchist, if she had any money, if she had a job, and with whom and how she was going to get there. If the immigration service of more than 100 years ago could process (handwritten in longhand) one million immigrants a year with a population of seventy million in the whole country, it seems to me we should be able to do a better job of it today. This was an America before databases and bureaucracies; we should be able to do at least as good of a job today.

The entire discussion of immigration these days is fueled by the concerns over national security that have been intensified by the attacks on 9/11. The bottom line is that we must know who is coming and going in this country. We have an immigration policy that is being largely ignored. In a post-9/11 world, the wink and a nod attitude between the federal government, American employers—large and small—and illegal immigrants must stop for the security of our nation.

This is not about limiting immigration; it is about managing it. Immigration should meet the need for workers and uphold our standards of keeping families together. Some of the first immigration laws in our country came about in the late 1700s and early 1800s and were designed to keep the French out. It was believed that the French were trying to undermine our new republic. In the late 1800s, there were laws relating to the intention to become a permanent resident of the United States. When I looked at the census for my great-grandparents in New York state, they had to declare whether they intended to be in the United States permanently. That is what determined if my grandfather and his siblings were United States citizens.

There were few laws regarding immigration until 1924. In the Ellis Island immigration period in the early 1900s, more than one million immigrants per year were processed *by hand* through that entry point and through the handful of other ports of entry in the United States. As a percentage, that is a larger proportion of immigrants than we have today. The difference is that we didn't have social programs paid by tax dollars as we do now. People had to make their own way and speak English to go to school. Some would argue that this was harsh, but that immigrant population assimilated into the society more quickly than immigrants today do.

According to the House Caucus on Immigration, from 1924 until the 1970s, the immigration levels were lowered to 150,000–350,000 per year. In 1986, Ronald Reagan was convinced that if we gave a one-time amnesty to illegal immigrants in this country we could slow the tide of illegal immigration. From that point on, illegal immigration increased on our southern border every year. Every time an American president even mentions the concept of amnesty, even if he doesn't use the word, illegal immigration across our border spikes.

It is estimated today that there are 8–20 million illegal immigrants in this country. If we closed and sealed the borders today, we would still have to deal with this problem. In August of 2001, President Bush and President Vicente Fox of Mexico met to discuss border normalization. President Fox made it clear in several speeches and in an interview with Sean Hannity and Alan Colmes on the Fox News Channel that he not only did not respect American sovereignty, but that America needed young Mexican workers to pay into the Social Security system. He would not even admit that people who crossed the border illegally were breaking the law.

On the heels of that visit and 9/11, the mood of this country changed dramatically. I am fully convinced that had there not been the attacks on America, the Bush administration would have pushed through an open borders policy with Mexico. In January 2004, President Bush unveiled his plan for immigration reform. His plan was based on five principles as outlined by the White House:

Protecting the Homeland by Controlling Our Borders: The program should link to efforts to control our border through agreements with countries whose nationals participate in the program. It must support ongoing efforts to enhance homeland security.

Serve America's Economy by Matching a Willing Worker with a Willing Employer: When no American worker is available and willing to take a job, the program should provide a labor supply for American employers. It should do so in a way that is clear, streamlined, and efficient so people can find jobs and employers can find workers in a timely manner.

Promoting Compassion: The program should grant currently working undocumented aliens a temporary worker status to prevent exploitation. Participants would be issued a temporary worker card that will allow them to travel back and forth between their home and the U.S. without fear of being denied re-entry into America.

Providing Incentives for Return to Home Country: The program will require the return of temporary workers to their home country after their period of work has concluded. The legal status granted by this program would last three years, be renewable, and would have an end. During the temporary work period, it should allow movement across the U.S. borders so the worker can maintain roots in their home country.

Protecting the Rights of Legal Immigrants: The program should not connect participation to a green card or citizenship. However, it should not preclude a participant from obtaining green card status through the existing process. It should not permit undocumented workers to gain an advantage over those who have followed the rules.

On the day the president unveiled his plan, I was asked to appear on CNN and comment on the plan before it was announced. I am glad the president put the discussion on the table, and I have supported a guest worker program for years. The only way a guest worker program will work, however, is to have the workers go back to their home countries, obtain guest worker visas, and then re-enter the country as legal immigrants.

Immigration control is inextricably tied to the 9/11 attacks. The hijackers on that day had more than sixty driver's licenses from several states at the time of the attack. Driver's licenses and the other documents of our society are keys for terrorists to easily access our country. In the final days of the 2004 congressional legislative session, the driver's license issue was taken out of the intelligence bill generated from the 9/11 Commission Report with the promise that it would be taken up in the new session. To get the support of James Sensenbrenner on the Intelligence Committee on the passage and acceptance of the recommendations from the 9/11 Commission Report, the White House had to promise to allow Sensenbrenner to bring up the driver's license issue as the first bill in the next Congress. It was brought up and was passed as the Real ID Bill and dramatically tightens the criteria for getting a driver's license in the United States. This passage was a big win for the legal immigration movement.

The day after the State of the Union, I talked with Tom DeLay, Republican majority leader of the House, about immigration and the president's guest worker program. He said,

> We have to protect our border . . . we have to enforce the law, but we also have to face the reality of ten to twenty million illegal immigrants in this country. How do you get them to go home and yet be able to face the reality that a man is going to come across this border if that's the only way he can feed his family? So, I'm one of those that really believes that we can give them incentive to go home by having a guest worker program that says you have to apply to the guest worker program from your country of origin. So you go home, you apply, you come in, you work, you don't bring your family in, you pay taxes so that there are some functions and facilities that the government provides you, you are least paying for them.

He went on to say, "You don't reward someone for breaking our laws." If that is the case, I can buy into this. It is a privilege to have the opportunity to live, work, and pay taxes in the United States. It is a privilege to be a United States citizen, and we need to start treating that privilege with respect.

Along with that respect, it is the responsibility of the United States government to establish English as our official language. While is it a gift to be able to get documents in your native language, once you become a citizen you should understand that all government documents will be in English, including election ballots. In many elections across the United States of America, ballots are offered in many different languages. The Voting Rights Act renewals over the years include a requirement to provide ballots in languages other than English if more than 5 percent of the voting population of that area speaks those languages as their first language. Adding that provision is a perversion of what the Voting Rights Act was designed to do, which was to provide voting rights to African Americans, who had been denied this right for many years.

You must be proficient in English to become a citizen and you must be able to vote in English. Any official document generated by a government of the United States of America should be in English. If it is an official document from a state of the United States of America or from the federal government, it should be in English. English is the language of the United States of America. It is the language of success in the world business community and must be protected from being diluted any further.

Most people agree with this, especially among the naturalized citizens in this country who came here the old-fashioned way—legally. They are proud of speaking English and worked hard to be able to do so. I had a caller recently who told me his child was sent home with Spanish language documents from school because he has a Latino surname. He is an immigrant but has spoken English for most of his life. Neither his children nor his wife speak Spanish at all. The assumption that people do not speak or understand English based on their appearance or their name should never happen. This type of discrimination is no different from what we fought so hard to stop in this country, and it should cease.

So what is the solution to this problem? First, secure the borders by whatever means necessary. Since we are going to be in the deserts of Iraq and Afghanistan for a while and we have conducted training exercises for the military on the border, then we should do more training of our military on the border to help guard and patrol it. This protects the military from becoming merely police on the border, but also serves as a deterrent.

Second, implement a guest worker program that requires illegal immigrants to go back to their home countries and apply for a guest worker visa. Driver's licenses will be given only to immigrants with a verifiable, valid status and will expire when the visa expires.

Third, serious penalties must be levied on employers who employ undocumented workers, including in the construction and hospitality industry. Allow employers and state welfare workers to verify documentation through a database they can access with immigrant information.

Fourth, we must give local law enforcement more jurisdiction over illegal immigrants in their own communities. Illegal immigrants who commit crimes must be tried in American courts and, if convicted, serve their entire sentences in American prisons. This seems on the surface to be harsh, but there is no evidence that their home governments, particularly Mexico, will prosecute them, and deportation will result in an unstoppable revolving door of violent crime in America. This is especially true with gang activity. The growth of gangs, which are primarily Latino, cannot be allowed and must be crushed with the full force of American law enforcement. Gangs are terrorists in our borders and cannot be allowed to flourish.

Lastly, immigrants must learn respect for their adopted American culture and the customs of this country by learning to speak English, the majority language of this country. I am the grandchild of an immigrant who kept and treasured the customs and traditions of the native land while also embracing the American culture. Immigrants who do not want to do this should not be able to benefit from our way of life and our freedoms.

Immigration policies should be enforced. We should support immigration, but it needs to be *legal* immigration. American taxpayers have been more than generous with their time, talents, and hard-earned dollars. There is no government without the taxpayers, and the taxpayers insist on a certain level of respect for America, for American culture, and for the laws that provide an unprecedented amount of freedom for American citizens. We do not want to be viewed as an unlimited cash cow that owes the world a living. We are a generous country and there is no society that will do more to help hard-working people be successful, but immigrants have to enter and exit our country legally and respect our culture and our laws while they are here. And if they decide to stay permanently and gain citizenship, they should understand that they swore an oath as an American citizen and, while honoring their home culture, should adopt and respect American culture.

I believe in immigration to the United States. We have a rich tradition of opening our arms to the people of the world. But we must never forget it is a privilege to come and live and work in the United States. It is not a right.

CHAPTER NINE

The War on Terror

Our war on terror begins with al Qaeda, but it does not end there. It will not end until every terrorist group of global reach has been found, stopped, and defeated.... Our response involves far more than instant retaliation and isolated strikes. Americans should not expect one battle, but a lengthy campaign, unlike any other we have ever seen. It may include dramatic strikes, visible on TV, and covert operations, secret even in success. We will starve terrorists of funding, turn them one against another, drive them from place to place, until there is no refuge or no rest.

—President George W. Bush, September 20, 2001

On the morning of September 11, 2001, I was scheduled to moderate a debate on my radio show between no-growth and pro-growth elected officials. This is always a controversial topic with heated positions on each side. The officials were waiting in WDUN's lobby. Leading up to the top of the hour and the beginning of the debate, my co-host Andy Maddox and I were considering the issues when I looked up to see what was on one of the TVs we use to follow the weather, state, and national news during the broadcast. I saw there was a fire in one of the World Trade Center towers and reported that to my audience as we went to a break. By the time the break was over, our station had gone to network coverage of a plane that had crashed into the World Trade Center towers.

When I was in New York in the mid 1980s I went to the top of the World Trade Center towers. Looking down from the towers was like looking down from an airplane. As I looked toward Brooklyn, New York, there was a fire in one of the neighborhoods. I watched as the fire trucks responded, feeling odd that I was watching someone else's tragedy unfold below me. As I watched the first tower burn on the morning of 9/11, I had that same feeling, but it was much worse. In my wildest imagination, I would not have predicted what came next. September 11, 2001, was a nightmare for those who make their living protecting this country.

People began to gather in the control room to watch. The politicians who were usually at odds and most of the people in the office were standing there as we saw the other plane come around and strike the second tower. There was a collective gasp. Andy Maddox was on the phone trying to reach his brother, who was in a meeting in the World Trade Center that morning. I went to my desk to try to call a friend of mine who lived in Manhattan. Andy found out later in the day that his brother had walked out of the building not five minutes before the first plane hit.

My friend was part of a ballet company whose studio was near the World Trade Center. She lived in Brooklyn, and I knew she came into Manhattan every day through the World Trade Center subway station. I tried all day to get her and several days later found out she had met up with most of the company members after the strikes and had walked all the way to Harlem, where one of them had an apartment. Many of the teenage students in the company were from other countries and were terrified. As they walked the more than 100 city blocks toward Harlem, they tried to get news from stores they passed. In Bob Seger's song "Against the Wind," he sings, "Wish I didn't know now what I didn't know then." I used to think I would give anything to be in a September 10th world, but we have to face adversity and learn from it. We have to grow up. This generation lost its innocence on 9/11 just as our parents' and grandparents' generation lost its innocence in the attack on Pearl Harbor.

Fairly early in the coverage of that day, I learned that a media colleague, Barbara Olsen, was in the plane that hit the Pentagon. By that time we had returned to local coverage and had taken calls into the afternoon. In our area we had two people who were in the Pentagon and were lost. Every family in America has been touched by this tragedy.

These people were not military targets. Even the people at the Pentagon were mostly bureaucrats, not soldiers. At Logan, Dulles, and Newark airports, innocent people boarded planes for different reasons, not knowing terrorists were going to take over the planes and use them as missiles. These people were going to work, going home, or going on vacation and they were used as pawns in a sick game of "gotcha."

Bill Maher, the comedian of *Politically Incorrect* fame, was criticized for saying that what the terrorists did in flying a plane into buildings was not cowardly, but even after his apology he had it wrong. Ashley Smith, the unlikely heroine of the Fulton County Court House shootings in March of 2005, said to Brian Nichols, the perpetrator of these brutal killings, that it took more of a man to face up to what he did than it takes to be killed by the police in a stand-off. This lady understood more than media-savvy comedian Maher. The terrorists were cowards. They could not face fighting law enforcement or the military to make their point. They killed innocent women, men, and children. The heroes of that day were the men and women who gave their lives, the brave first responders in these attacked cities, and the American people.

In preparation to write this chapter, I reread the 9/11 Commission Report. The minute-by-minute account of the day they pieced together was chilling, and as I read it, I began to feel sick as I relived those moments. There is a Darryl Worley song that was written during the first phase of the war on terror in Afghanistan. He was visiting there and got the idea for the song "Have You Forgotten?" One of the verses says the following:

> They took all the footage off my T.V.
> Said it's too disturbing for you and me
> It'll just breed anger that's what the experts say
> If it was up to me I'd show it every day

Some say this country's just out looking for a fight
After 9/11, man, I'd have to say that's right.

That's how I feel about the 9/11 report. We should all read it again and again. I don't read it for the analysis or the testimony. I read it for the first few sections that pull together what happened that day and remind us of what we are fighting for.

The president told us from the beginning that this is a war that may last beyond his time in office. He warned us there would be good days and bad days, days we would hear about the victories and days we would hear about defeats. The president laid out the plan for this fight for our civilization, and he has told the truth about what to expect. If you really listened to that speech to a joint session of Congress on September 20, 2001, then you can understand what we have done and where we are going with this protection of our society. Most days we have done a good job fighting the war on terror in Afghanistan and Iraq. The only days that worry me are the days it appears politicians, not military leaders, are calling the shots—days like those around the battle for Fallujah.

George W. Bush is right that the only way to squash this kind of activity is to have democracy break out all over the Middle East. We have seen already that those who have said that some people can't govern themselves are wrong. They said it about the colonists in the New World and were wrong. They said it about the eastern Europeans who were under Communist control for so many years and were wrong. They are wrong today as well. There will always be voices of doom and despair in the world and many of them write for the liberal newspapers of the United States of America. It is amazing that the soldiers, who are fighting and dying in conflicts all over the world, fight for the right for people to say what they think, even if it is to blame America first.

In 2005, Muslim professors from Kabul University in Afghanistan came to America with an exchange program to learn more about America. They were surprised by the positive way they were received in cities all across America and they were impressed with the open and respectful way Muslims were allowed to practice their religion. They said they didn't know that about America and they would take the message of how America really is back to their home country. We are making progress and it would be amazing how much progress we could make around the world if our own press would actually report things the way they are in America.

Since we went into Afghanistan, its citizens have begun to form a free and democratic government. Iraq has had free and democratic elections for the first time in their long history. Qatar is moving toward a constitutional monarchy on its own. Saudi Arabia is holding local elections. Libya is cooperating and dismantling its weapons programs. Lebanon is fighting peacefully for its ability to govern itself. There is democracy breaking out all over the world and when the light of freedom shines, then the evil of terrorism is harder to propagate. But we must be aware that terrorism can never be completely ended. It has been a part of history and will be a part of our future.

For instance, the terrorism we are fighting today is not much different from the terrorism we fought on the high seas in the early 1800s under the presidency of Thomas Jefferson. After our independence was won, Congress followed the European tradition of paying a tribute of $80,000 to the Barbary pirates. This payment was to allow free passage on the high seas. This practice was not unlike the "protection" money you see depicted in Mafia movies. The Barbary pirates wanted money in return for a promise not to take sailors and cargo from American ships. In 1784, Thomas Jefferson and John Adams began negotiations with the pirates (terrorists of the seas in those days) to end the tributes to the Barbary pirates. It seems like some truths hold true in 1784 as in 2004; you can't negotiate with terrorists because the next year, Algerian pirates (the Barbary Coast was in Algeria—thus Barbary pirates) captured two American ships. The governor of Algiers held their crews of twenty-one people for a ransom of nearly $60,000.

Jefferson believed that paying the demands would only lead to further demands. In letters to John Adams and James Monroe, Jefferson said, "I acknolege [sic] I very early thought it would be best to effect a peace thro' the medium of war." In another letter, Jefferson said, "Paying tribute will merely invite more demands, and even if a coalition proves workable, the only solution is a strong navy that can reach the pirates." He went on to say, "The states must see the rod; perhaps it must be felt by some one of them. . . . Every national citizen must wish to see an effective instrument of coercion, and should fear to see it on any other element than the water. A naval force can never endanger our liberties, nor occasion bloodshed; a land force would do both." Then to Ezra Stiles, president of Yale College, Jefferson wrote, "From what I learn from the temper of my countrymen and their tenaciousness of their money, it will be more easy to raise ships and men to fight these pirates into reason, than money to bribe them."

By 1801, Jefferson was proven right when the Barbary pirates demanded $225,000 from Congress for "protection" that year. For the next fifteen years, there were wars with the Barbary pirates, until naval victories by Commodores William Bainbridge and Stephen Decatur led to treaties ending all tribute payments by the United States. Europeans continued to pay the tributes until the 1830s. Terrorism has been around for a long time, and state-sponsored terrorist groups like the Barbary pirates and Al Qaeda are the most difficult to fight. But as the president said in our time and as Jefferson alluded to in his, it is the responsibility of free men to fight for the rights of others in order to make the world a better place.

When the Coalition Provisional Authority turned power over to the Iraqi provisional governments on June 28, 2004, the president was passed a note and he scribbled on it, "Freedom is on the March." At first blush, it sounded like Bushism. For some reason it didn't sound quite right, but after hearing the president use that phrase in many other venues where he spoke about the success in the war on terror, it seems to fit him and what he is doing for our country.

Bush did not ask for this war, but he has handled it well. As he said on September 20, 2001, to the joint session of Congress in the aftermath of the attacks,

This war will not be like the war against Iraq a decade ago, with a decisive liberation of territory and a swift conclusion. It will not look like the air war above Kosovo two years ago, where no ground troops were used and not a single American was lost in combat. Our response involves far more than instant retaliation and isolated strikes. Americans should not expect one battle, but a lengthy campaign, unlike any other we have ever seen. It may include dramatic strikes, visible on TV, and covert operations, secret even in success. We will starve terrorists of funding, turn them one against another, drive them from place to place, until there is no refuge or no rest. And we will pursue nations that provide aid or safe haven to terrorism. Every nation, in every region, now has a decision to make. Either you are with us, or you are with the terrorists. From this day forward, any nation that continues to harbor or support terrorism will be regarded by the United States as a hostile regime.

President Bush laid out the costs of the war on terror, and he has stayed that course. As much as his political enemies tried to demonize him in the 2004 election and called him a liar, the people didn't believe them. They believed the president and they gave him a political victory that mandated that he should stay the course on the war on terror. This is the issue of our time. The only way to win this war is to continue to fight to spread freedom throughout the world. Sometimes it does take might to make right.

CHAPTER TEN

On Tour in Iraq:
The New Media and Our
War on Terror

Our families and the people back home, yea, they're behind us . . . the American people are 90–95 percent behind us. For the 5–10 percent in America that aren't behind us, I feel we should tell them that if you don't like the way we live, why don't you go to different country and live under a dictatorship and a tyrant and see if that doesn't change your opinion?
— First Sgt. Eugene Dufrene, Mississippi National Guard,
Baghdad, Iraq, July 2005

I have been trying to get to Iraq or Afghanistan since the beginning of the war in October 2002. As more stories—some good, some bad—came out of the theater of operation, I wanted to go all the more. I knew from my years of talking to people everywhere I go that the number of good stories must outweigh the bad.

So when my good friend Lt. Col Buzz Patterson called me with an invitation to travel to Iraq with other radio talk show hosts on the "Voices of Soldiers" Truth Tour, I accepted immediately. Retired after more than twenty years with the United States Air Force, Buzz is a real American hero, a well-known author, and a long-time fan of Fox 5 Atlanta's *The Georgia Gang*. What he was offering me was the chance to talk to soldiers on the ground in the war on terror, thank them for their service, and then find out how *they* think this war is going, and I couldn't refuse the opportunity. Buzz explained that he would work with Move America Forward (an issues-oriented conservative organization that also develops projects to support the troops) on the trip details and that he was having daily discussions with CENTCOM (Central Command Headquarters) on how to organize and proceed.

While there is no one I would rather have interaction with than members of the United States Armed Services, I understand that the higher up the ladder you get, the more bureaucracy you have to deal with—or I should say, that Buzz Patterson had to deal with. Over the next few weeks, the dates were made and changed; details were confirmed and changed and reconfirmed. Finally, on June 3, 2005, we had a "go" on the trip. Our group would first go to CENTCOM in Tampa for briefing. After that, we had to get our group to Kuwait and then take a military transport into Iraq.

Pre-Trip Problems

We began to encounter obstacles to our trip between our initial approval on June 3 and July 7, the day we'd head to Tampa for the first leg of the trip. The Move America Forward press release started the ball rolling and began a smoldering among the Left in this country, especially the left-wing media. Several times, the trip was nearly cancelled because of bad publicity the week before we were scheduled to leave. Once our trip was announced, the media, who are certainly more left-leaning than the country at large, began making assumptions. Before the first word was written from the field or a broadcast was made, the Left said we were unfit to report from a war zone. The irony of this charge is that there are never any questions about the way writers or other journalists report from Iraq. If it's a positive message, it's automatically discounted.

A great example of liberal reaction to our trip came July 6, 2005. Peter Beinart, editor of left-wing *The New Republic*, said, "This is the most pathetic thing I've heard in a long time. They should be ashamed of themselves. . . . They have no idea what journalism is, and to pretend they are journalists is laughable." He went on to say, "You do not achieve victory by not facing reality. I think these are the kinds of people who will lead us to lose there." He said this before we wrote a word or started a broadcast. I thought the Left didn't like to make stereotypical snap judgments about people.

Just a month before, Ellen Ratner of Talk Radio News Service had escorted a group to Iraq with no air of criticism. Ellen is also a liberal commentator for the Fox News Channel and is an honest liberal. I don't agree with a single thing she concludes from her research, but I respect where she comes from and believe that we arrive at different conclusions. I would never say she was unable to come to a particular conclusion because she is a liberal; I would just say she was wrong.

Talk Radio as "Real" Journalism

Talk radio is much maligned as not being "real" journalism. Before we left, there were attacks on our credibility, questions about our credentials, implications that we were using tax dollars to fund our trip, and assertions that because we were right-wingers, we would be unable to report fairly. I would argue that I have higher standards than the average *New York Times* columnist, reporter, or editor. I am a graduate of the University of Georgia Grady School of Journalism, which is one of the most prestigious journalism schools in the country.

The rest of our group also had years of experience in radio, television, newspapers, and film. It included Buzz Patterson of RightTalk; Melanie Morgan of KSFO in San Francisco; Mark Williams of KFBK in Sacramento and producer Holly Williams; Michael Graham of WMAL in Washington, DC; Howard Kaloogian of Move America Forward; Brad Maaske of KMJ in Fresno (an expert on Saddam Hussein); filmmaker Dan Hare; Navy and commercial pilot, 9/11 family member Marc Flagg; Nancy Alexander;

Move America Forward former executive director Sioban Guiney; and me, Martha Zoller of WDUN and RightTalk. We didn't come from the small area in Manhattan that houses the executives of most of the major news networks. I don't hobnob with the beautiful people in New York, Los Angeles, or Washington, DC. I love all those cities, but the viewpoints that are put forth there as "American" views don't pass the test of the mainstream. These large cities of the media elite simply aren't mainstream conservative Middle America, where most of Americans live, work, and play.

Our group went to Iraq with the presupposition that the war on terror is going better than is being reported. According to some people, that made us unfit to report on what we saw. How is that any different than Peter Beinart going into a war zone with the assumption that the war is going badly? The truth is, there is no difference. Every journalist goes into a story with some assumptions; that's how the idea for a story originates, but a good journalist will assess whether the information fits the assumptions.

Although I said previously that I don't believe in stereotyping an entire group of people, liberals believe the New Media (talk radio, bloggers, and the like) are incapable of discerning the nuances of the issue. The fact of the matter is that conservative talk show hosts like me are more honest about their conclusions and their audience's ability to discern bias. I freely admit I have a bias and go to great lengths to give voice to the other side. The admission of bias allows my listeners to know where I come from on issues. The liberal, mainstream media will never admit their bias, so they are dishonest going into *any* discussion of an issue.

Our only goal was to get the truth out from soldiers. Captain Daniel Green, stationed in the Green Zone/International Zone (best known as the Green Zone, but the Iraqis and Americans now refer to it as the International Zone), said, "I can't think of anything more truthful than soldiers rubbing stuffed animals for luck before a mission. Or soldiers telling a cameraman that morale is down, or showing off an orphanage that we frequent. . .nothing you saw was damaging or put soldiers in harm's way." Capt. Green saw the trip as we did, as an opportunity to hear the stories both good and bad.

Why It Matters

I am going to take some time to go through the substance of the trip, look at the press that was attributed to the trip, and then point out the obvious: liberals believe they alone can be objective about world events.

I have a more personal reason why I do small things and big things for our military servicemen and women. I do what I do for the military in our country for two reasons: they are my heroes who protect our freedom and defend our way of life around the country, and I wish to honor the memory of my father, Frank A. Mitchell, who was a WWII veteran and POW. He died in 1991, and at his funeral, Fort Jackson sent an honor guard to present the flag and to play "Taps." There is not a day that goes by that I don't think about him. In a strange way, this war and the projects I have done for the military and their families bring me closer to the part of my father's life that I only heard about. I get so much more out of serving military folks than I give. If a blessing can come out of adversity, I have found my silver lining in understanding a little more about my father, the military, and this country he loved so much. I am the patriot I am today because of him. He was the one who taught me to stand and sing the National Anthem, and he was the one who taught me to shake the hand of anyone in uniform. He was the one who taught me to defend America even in adversity.

On Our Way

The "Voices of Soldiers" Truth Tour arrived at CENTCOM in Tampa as a kind of "red-headed stepchild." We had permission to go, but after the minor outburst of bad publicity, CENTCOM received a few calls from liberal groups who were worried that taxpayers were funding a propaganda trip. Then CENTCOM got calls from within the government that concerned the mid-level officers. I certainly understand it—if I had read what was written about us, I would have been wary too. CENTCOM wanted to be sure that there would be no politics in our trip. Politics was never the intent, but now we had to prove that the tour was about the soldiers. For me, the trip was never about anything else. I have been around the military enough to know that they reflect society, and there are as many different personal views in the military as there are in the civilian world. In the work I do, I don't want to alienate any soldier, sailor, airman, or marine.

As you would expect, Tampa in July is hot. On that hot and humid Friday at CENTCOM, our group was on display. We had about six hours to convince General Abaziad and his staff that they should support the trip and allow us not only to go to Kuwait, but also to Baghdad.

We began the day with a briefing by General John Custer and colleagues about the war on terror. This was an unclassified report, and I kept thinking, "Why isn't this on every TV screen in America?" After the briefing, it was clear the military understands the scope of the threat and has a strategy to defeat it. This presentation of the wins/losses and strategies supported the statements that the President has made all along this journey regarding the successes we see *and* the successes we don't see. The key component is the cooperation of the moderate Muslim world.

General Custer went into great detail in his discussion of all the aspects of terrorism and how we are fighting it with our coalition partners. There are more than 180 countries in the United Nations, and there are 90 countries represented in the coalition of the war on terror. Some may help with terrorism, with Iraq, or with Afghanistan (or all three), but half the world is truly behind us, committing resources, time, talent, or troops. Most of the world is with us on this important mission. A striking symbol of this unified effort is the number of country flags flying in Coalition City at CENTCOM

Public Relations and the Human Face of Our Mission

In April 2005, I had the opportunity to participate in the Joint Civilian Orientation Conference (JCOC). This conference is the oldest civilian/military interaction in the Department of Defense.

One of the most important things I brought away from that meeting was the realization that there are many resources available to the American people to help them find out what's happening in the war on terror; we just have to work to get that message to the American people (much like the communication machine in World War II got the word out). Both military and civilians must tout the successes of the war on terror because the mainstream media is focused only on the wins of the terrorist insurgents.

I have been turning over in my mind scenarios where civilian marketers, promoters, and others in the publicity business could serve their country by aiding in getting this message out. Whether it is getting the unclassified version of our briefing out to the public or raising awareness about the huge amount of information available on the Department of Defense websites, there is a role for the private sector to play in this war. Anyone who works in any kind of communications or in public relations owes it to this country to offer their services to promote the war effort. For too long we have acted like our country owes us. We owe it to America to give everything we have when times are bad because she gives us the ability to live free in this society every day.

One of the things our group was criticized for was organizing a lunch to thank all the people at CENTCOM for their hard work on behalf of this country and its citizens. We did what any group would do to get servicepeople to show up to talk to us: we gave them free food. When we arrived on Thursday, July 7, we learned there were about a thousand people working in their Area of Responsibility (AOR) at CENTCOM and that we would be lucky if half that many showed up. Our group, with sponsor Stafford Hospitality, provided a barbeque lunch for 600 people—and we ran out of food with many more servicemen and women to feed. I know the old saying is "leave them wanting more," but I never want to see a hungry soldier.

During the barbeque lunch we each got up and explained why we had come. Our stories were important because the folks needed to hear why we were there, but Marc Flagg's story that epitomized our most important purpose. Marc's parents, Bud and Dee Flagg, were on American Airlines Flight 77 when it crashed into the Pentagon on

September 11. Marc described how his parents' deaths had changed his life; he talked about his tireless work on airline security issues since then and about his own service in the United States Navy. Marc Flagg didn't *want* to become an airline security expert. He didn't *want* to be working day and night for securing cargo or arming pilots; it is because of September 11 and the loss of his parents that he does this important work. While most of us were broadcasting on Friday, Marc worked the "chow line" and shook hands and thanked the soldiers. He became the face of this mission for me because I would have never been in Iraq if there hadn't been a 9/11. Seeing the reality of 9/11 in Marc Flagg was one of the best things about this trip. For many of these soldiers, Marc's gratitude for their service to our country was emotionally overwhelming. Whether they work behind a desk at CENTCOM or on the field of battle, the folks we fed that day are protecting us from terrorism and preserving our way of life.

When we got back to the hotel that night in Tampa, we felt that we had convinced CENTCOM that the liberal media and the leftists groups who said we were political hacks were wrong. By the next morning, when we left for Kuwait, we had our transport to Baghdad secured and the escorts we needed to make the trip a success.

From Kuwait to Baghdad

We had little access to news or Internet until we arrived in Kuwait City, and even there access was limited. When one of us would find a story written about the trip, we would print it if we could and pass it around. As the trip got underway and we began to broadcast, stories about our "slant" were replaced by reports of what we were doing— talking uncensored to soldiers, sailors, airmen, and marines.

Kuwait City was filled with lights. As the week went on and we saw areas of Iraq without reliable electricity, it became clear that the bright lights of Kuwait City were a sign of wealth and stability. When we checked in to our hotel, the only hotel we would stay in for the trip, we were issued bullet-proof vests and helmets. Despite the protective gear, my colleagues and I weren't fearful during this trip. But when we headed to the air base in Kuwait the next day on the way to Baghdad, we wore the vests and helmets.

Buzz Patterson and Marc Flagg are pilots, so even in the spartan surroundings of a C130 air transport plane they were excited about being on a military airplane again. It was too loud to talk, so I spent my time watching the soldiers and marines who were on the flight with us. These guys were going to war—some for the first time, some returning from leave or for a second or third tour. It was clear they were going to war. Sitting on the webbed seats in full gear, they passed the time on the flight to Baghdad listening to music or talking or sleeping. We landed doing what is called a combat landing. It is a sort of spiral landing where the plane descends quickly, moving side to side to make the plane less of a target. During our landing, there were armed soldiers practically hanging out of the side doors, prepared to take offensive and defensive action if necessary. I think flares were fired. I'm not certain at what or why—but there was a very loud noise that made some of us wonder if we were going to be fired on today.

We arrived at Baghdad Airport in what appeared to be a military section. We were loaded on a bus with our group. Captain Suzanne Ovel was the Public Affairs Officer assigned to us. We wanted to broadcast that day, but she didn't have the additional phone lines that we needed. With a little flexibility and "American ingenuity," we made it work. The preferred method of transmission is ISDN telephone line, which is available in most (but not all) of the United States. (In addition to WDUN in Georgia, I work with RightTalk, which is based out of Wyoming. I had to laugh because they can't even get ISDN in Wyoming, so how did we expect to get it in Iraq?) I had made the arrangements ahead of time to have a co-host, Al Gainey, in the studio to cover if there were any terminal technical problems, but despite the sand and lack of ISDN lines, we all eventually made our broadcasts with only a few problems. They did have phone lines, and Sgt. Ernie Paquette back at CENTCOM to patch the calls through to our stations.

When we arrived at Camp Victory in Baghdad, we were shown to our tents and cots. I brought a sheet and some of us brought sleeping bags, but the accommodations were as austere as I expected. The tent was three layers thick and zipped up in every imaginable place. However, in addition to the wood floor, there was power, air conditioning, and a wireless internet connection in the tent, so we were pretty comfortable. That night, I used my flak jacket as a pillow, stored my gear under the cot, and had a pretty good night's sleep. The tent had room for twenty women, and there were soldiers and marines who were temporarily housed there as they were going from one assignment to another. The randomness of who was in the tent meant that I had a variety of information sources. I didn't formally interview the women in the tent, but I did talk to them. I wanted them to be relaxed with me and look at me as a bunkmate, not a journalist.

During that first night, some of my colleagues listened to part of an Air America Radio broadcast. The host of the show and a guest were talking about us and said we were probably sitting out by the pool sipping adult beverages in Kuwait. That would have been nice, but there was no pool, and there were definitely no adult beverages. Again the same media sources (and calling Air America a media source is a stretch) who said we had already formed our conclusions about the war's progress and therefore couldn't report fairly were making incorrect assumptions about what we were doing in Iraq. When I returned to America, my publicist sent a pitch to Air America so I could correct their perception that we really didn't go into Iraq and really didn't live with the troops, but they never responded.

Briefings and Interviews

The next day we were able to talk to the general of the Iraqi Army, Lt. General Abdul Qader Jassim, who gave a short statement and then took questions from our group. The only prohibited questions were questions about Iraqi or U.S. operational details. He spoke in Arabic with his interpreter and an interpreter from the United States Army. He described his training in the USSR and told us through an interpreter that Russian was his second language. He appeared to understand what we said, but he answered in Arabic. He likened the regime of Saddam Hussein to gangs, gangsters and the Mafia and said that the coalition was fighting the regime of Saddam Hussein—not the Iraqi people. He was clear that the Iraqi Army had been decimated after the first Gulf War and that the country had been run by the Baathists, what was left of the Republican Guard, and a regime of gangs. He made the correlation to gangs many times in our presentation. He was complimentary to the Coalition Forces and the progress being made, but he did worry about public support in America and spoke directly to that.

There were two big revelations in this briefing. First, we learned that there were four thousand terrorists living in Iraq at the time of the invasion of Afghanistan, and they were given safe harbor in Iraq, including food, shelter, medical and training assistance. Lt. General Abdul Qader said that he had participated in training terrorists to be used against Iraq's enemies in Lebanon and Syria. He reiterated that while Iraq may have been more "stable" under Saddam that stability in fear is worthless. He emphasized that the people now have hope, and they didn't have hope under the regime of Saddam Hussein. He also talked about the challenges of recruiting an army—that initially they were looking for quantity, but now they are looking for quality. It is also interesting that some of protesting that takes place outside of the Green Zone/International Zone is by Iraqi men who *want* to join the army; they are protesting to get *in* the army. I bet we won't hear that story on the six o'clock news.

Lt. General Abdul Qader admitted that there are problems, but he seems aware of them and is in the process of fixing them. He acknowledged that there is corruption in some of the processes, such as in army hiring practices, among others. One persistent problem has been the Iraqi army's level of readiness. Overall, he estimated that two divisions are 80 percent ready and that the others are between 20-40 percent ready. He believes that the Iraqi army could secure the country on its own in two years.

The second major revelation occurred when Michael Graham asked him why someone didn't tell Saddam that he couldn't beat the coalition. Lt. General Abdul Qader said, "You mean tell Saddam

Hussein...?" After the laughter subsided, he said that he had made a report to his superiors before the first Gulf War in 1991 that their tanks were no match for the Americans' Abrams tanks. When the war was over and Iraq had lost, Abdul Qader was in and out of jail for seven years, and his military career was effectively over while Saddam Hussein remained in power. This man lived under Saddam and worked for him. He was a career officer who had been groomed under the Soviet system. He said terrorism had to be defeated in the streets of Iraq so there would not be more metro station bombings in London. It was clear he knows what the future of Iraq is and he wants to be a part of it. (You can access the full audio of the interview with Abdul Qader at www.marthazoller.com.)

After our briefing with Lt. General Abdul Qader, we had a companion briefing with Col. Ben Hodges. He talked more about the transitions of troops and troop draw down, and he answered our questions. It was a very informal briefing where we were able to ask questions. He gave similar answers regarding troop readiness and the falling back of the coalition forces when the Iraqi Army is ready to take the lead. He also reiterated the commitment of George W. Bush and Donald Rumsfeld to do whatever it takes to complete the mission, regardless of public opinion. That was a message we heard everywhere. Coalition forces will go home when the Iraqis can handle their own security. He said he would be surprised if more troops were needed in Iraq by early 2006. I must tell you the soldiers on the ground were not that optimistic. The soldiers I talked to who were directly involved with the training of Iraqi forces were consistent in their assessments. They mostly believe that they will be able to stand down or serve in support roles in two years, but that the overall commitment to the region has to go on until the Iraqi democracy is secured.

One of my first on-air interviews with soldiers was with Captain Daniel Green. He is from Atlanta but is based out of Ft. Stewart while he fulfills his medical school requirement by serving as the chief medical officer for one of the units in the Green Zone/International Zone. He heard about us coming over and sought us out to tell his side of the story and the stories of his men.

His brigade and battalion wanted us to hear from him and the soldiers he take care of. What impressed me the most about Capt. Green is that his priority is the whole well-being of his men. He knew about his men, he kept track of them, and they knew they had a partner in him.

Other interviews included staff from the office and several soldiers from Georgia, Missouri, and Massachusetts. I talked to Pfc. Corey McClintic and Sgt. Matthew Kennedy from the 20th Engineers Brigade about the projects they worked on. Their project that week was a covered space for the motor pool so that when they had to fix humvees (which was every day), they only had to work in the heat, not the heat and sun. They also worked on water projects, and they figured out ways to divert some of their budget to projects designed to help Iraqi families.

We also talked to Kayla Eckert, a civilian employee with the Army Corps of Engineers, about projects funded with the billions appropriated by the United States for reconstruction of Iraq. But the real blessing was talking to the chief chaplain for Camp Victory, Col. Fr. Rutherford. He said his mission was to bring God to the soldiers and the soldiers to God. I thank God he's there. If there is any time a soldier needs God, it is in war. You won't hear the mainstream media talking about a military mission to bring God to the soldiers and the soldiers to God. It was ironic that we could hear the call to prayer in the background as we were leaving the chaplain's offices. It gave context to what we were doing. Finally, Col. Fr. Rutherford handed me a bulletin from a memorial service he had given for a female soldier. He does that for all the soldiers who die there. The bulletin was filled with stories from people who knew her, and the service offered an opportunity for soldiers to pay their respects. Respect for the mission, too, is something they have a lot of there.

Morale, Welfare, and Recreation

I came close to having an opportunity to ride on a helicopter early one morning, but a sandstorm came in and made that impossible. I am a firm believer that things happen for a reason. I was disappointed I didn't get out on a helicopter, and I was feeling sorry for myself. I used that opportunity to go by the MWR (Morale, Welfare, and Recreation) and talk to some soldiers. I met the most incredible people there from the Mississippi National Guard and later from the South Carolina National Guard. I was also able to talk to soldiers in the mess hall, and during the day I was in the camp, I broadcast from the Al Faz Palace. There I met soldiers from the Hawaiian National Guard, from my home state of Georgia, and from around the country. I talked to interpreters too. One was a Syrian woman who had lived in America all her life. She volunteered to come to Iraq as an Arab-speaking American citizen and help the soldiers and the Iraqis. There were many stories like that, and while my goal was to talk to soldiers, the stories of the contract workers were even more interesting. Most were former military who still had something to contribute even outside of the military structure. So, despite the technical glitches, all the broadcasts went well in Baghdad, and it was an incredible experience.

Questions of Morale

There really aren't words to describe the overall feeling in Iraq. It was humbling and rewarding. The soldiers, sailors, airmen, and marines were the best and the brightest that this nation has to offer. I read a report when I came home that the morale of the military in Iraq is at an all time low. I really don't know how we measure something like that. Are soldiers supposed to be happy to be there? We cannot forget that with the logistics of moving soldiers for one-year tours, marines with seven-month tours, and other personnel with three- to six-month tours, the military has moved as many men and women in and out of the theater as they did in World War II. That is a logistical nightmare, but we are doing it to maintain the morale of our troops.

I think that 1st Sgt. Eugene Dufrene summed it up when he explained that there are problems, but the soldiers figure out how to get people involved to fix them. I am proud of that sort of American ingenuity. The letters I have received from those deployed say being there is hard, but it's getting better. I think that's a plus for morale. I also think the morale question will be resolved as soldiers complete the mission. When they look back on what they accomplished in Iraq, when they are the age of the Greatest Generation, they will be the Greatest Generation of our time. I am more committed to the mission in Iraq than I was before. Failure of the mission is not an option for our freedom to be protected and to honor those who gave all in support of this mission.

Our Last Day

On the fourth day, we packed up in a sand storm, headed to the Baghdad Airport, and hoped for the best. It was the second day of the storm, and there was some question whether we would get out at all. We watched the Armed Forces Network, which characterized the storm as the worst in history. I joked that the storm would be blamed on the American presence in Iraq—all those extra emissions and heat. We spent eighteen hours in the Baghdad airport during the sand storm, but it was a wonderful opportunity to encounter a true cross-section of those serving in Iraq and to listen to many of their stories. I talked to a soldier who was going home on leave to take care of his wife after an operation. He was a guy who jumped out of planes—I'm not sure he was going to be able to sit still at home. We talked to teachers who were there to figure out how the army will teach new technology to new recruits. We talked to Special Ops guys who couldn't tell us what they did. It was a genuine cross-section of military, contractors, and civilians.

There were two people who were unforgettable. One was an American UN worker who spoke with an English accent. One of the big pushes of the political side of Move America Forward is the ousting of the United Nations, so Howard Kaloogian and a couple of other folks struck up a conversation with her. When the discussion got to the discussion of the July 12 car bomb that drove into a crowd of children who were being given candy and toys by an American soldier, she said, "Isn't is sad that the soldier was giving the kids candy?" We could not believe she blamed the soldier—not the suicide car bomber—for the bombing. First of all, everyone, especially soldiers, is anti-war. A soldier and regular email buddy from Iraq said, "Most soldiers, current and past, even if they disagree with the way we are doing things over here (in Iraq), know enough to keep their mouths shut as long as soldiers are in harm's way." That candor is what I love about soldiers, and that is the kind of respectful frankness we got all week.

The second person we met was a soldier in line with us at the Subway sandwich shop at the Baghdad Airport. Now, he wouldn't be a good soldier if he didn't complain a little bit, but he was complaining about everything—the food, calling cards back home, the pay—you name it. Then Dan Hare asked him what his job was. He told us it was his job to go get the bodies of dead Americans and bring them back in. Then we knew. He had the hardest and most thankless job in the military—the job no one wants to do. So we found him some phone cards and thanked him for his work. As Dan was leaving, he told him to be careful out there because if anything happens to him, "I'll be the one who has to come and get you."

From the job at the bottom to the four-star general, every man and woman in this military is important. Some have the good jobs; some just have necessary jobs, and others have the jobs that no one wants to do. That's why I came to Iraq, to meet them all.

Back to America

We finally got out and landed in Kuwait with just enough time to make it to the airport and miss our flight. Luckily there was another flight about thirty minutes later and we got on and headed back to the United States. I had been traveling forty-four hours by the time I got home; I was dirty, tired, and had been sick for most of the final leg of our journey. I really could have stayed longer, but at the same time I was ready to be home. I know I will go back; I know that making trips to where the soldiers are will be something I will do the rest of my life. We are so blessed to have this place as our home and to have been born in the United States. Like in the post-WWII era, there will be many battles to save this republic from the inside.

If you really know history, you know that we must be diligent in preserving the republic and our form of government. The next big outside threat is China; the biggest inside threat is unchecked illegal immigration. But our veterans will be equipped to handle all of these things because of their service. At the beginning of the film *The Passion of the Christ*, there is a Bible verse from the book of John: "Greater love has no one than this, that he lay down his life for his friends." There is no greater calling, and the men and women who are in service to our country are fulfilling this truth.

What I Brought Home

I learned four important things at CENTCOM, in Kuwait and in Iraq. First, I was impressed that General John Custer said we had to listen to our coalition partners because they have a perspective we can never have. They live outside of America and see the world in a way we who reside in this country cannot. The coalition is a true partnership where the members learn from one another.

Second, the National Guard is imminently equipped mentally and physically for the task at hand. In some areas, because they have worked together longer and their families know each other, they do certain things better than the regular army. I was also surprised to learn that the men, women, and families of the regular army do need more support. But when I consider the circumstances, this makes sense: the guardsmen are more mature; they live and work in the nonmilitary world, and they have stayed in the same unit for a number of years. A soldier moving up in "this man's army," relocates every two to four years. Such constant transition makes life much more difficult for these soldiers and their families. Because of this hardship, I am going to make it a priority to find more army families to take care of in the next year.

Third, the Iraqi people like us. They see that the path to freedom is through the coalition and the success of their own security forces. Especially after the July car bombing that killed so many children, the people cooperated more with the soldiers. After the London bombings, we started to see the kind of language coming out of the Muslim community that should have happened on September 12, 2001.

Finally, the coalition understands the threat and how to defeat it politically, economically, and militarily. Today's military knows they have to be creative to fight this war on all fronts. The sprawling Department of Defense doesn't like to change, but it must. When the transformation is complete, we will have an army that can meet our security needs throughout the world. The best example of this occurred last fall when there was a big push in Afghanistan. For a particular battle, sharp shooters were flown to Afghanistan from all over the country. They landed, fought for three days, won the battle, then went home. It was like a business trip. You will always need support on the ground, but the footprint won't have to be as big.

So this was our trip to Iraq. I would take any offer to go to Iraq, Afghanistan, or anywhere our soldiers, sailors, airmen, and marines are in harm's way. When I returned to the United States, I was glad to be home and even prouder to be an American. The bad press that that preceded our trip just wouldn't stick—the truth won out on the "Voices of Soldiers" Truth Tour. We brought back the good *and* the bad for the American people to decide for themselves—and they believed us because we were telling the truth about what we saw in Iraq.

CHAPTER ELEVEN

Tax Replacement, not Tax Reform

All roads lead to tax replacement.
> —Herman Cain, political activist and author of
> *They Think You're Stupid,* June 2004

Our current federal income tax was established in 1913. It required an amendment to the United States Constitution to make it legal. Our founding fathers believed taxing individuals on their private income would destroy the economy. History shows us that they were right. The absence of an income tax, an absurd tax on *productivity*, allowed our economy to grow and individuals to prosper for 124 years. Since the inception of federal income taxes, the strongest growth in our economy since then came at times when substantial cuts to tax rates were made.

The original legislation taxed earnings of $4,000 or more per year. The national average income in 1920 was $1,500 a year, so most Americans were exempt from income taxes. The 16th Amendment says, "The Congress shall have power to lay and collect taxes on incomes, from whatever source derived, without apportionment among the several States, and without regard to any census or enumeration." That's all it says on the subject. The first tax return was one page; the entire tax code consisted of only fourteen pages. Today the complete Internal Revenue Code contains more than 2.8

million words. Printed 60 lines to the page, it would fill almost 6,000 letter-size pages.

The only imaginable reason for this vast difference is that government and elected officials have to justify their existence. In fact, our society is not more complicated; government and elected officials have made it more complicated in order to stay in power. Initially Congress did not even meet the entire year. Now it is more than a full-time job for most congressmen. They become rich while they are in office and even more so afterward as lobbyists to the same government where they once worked.

The federal income tax system has become so complex that it requires tens of millions of Americans to seek professional help to comply with it, not to mention the enormous, expensive federal bureaucracy required to enforce and administer the tax. The Internal Revenue Service employs more investigative agents than the FBI and the CIA combined. One could argue that if we didn't have IRS investigators and took that money over the years and spent more time and money on intelligence gathering, we could have prevented the terrorist attacks on 9/11. Why in the world would we commit more resources to taking money from taxpayers than we would in protecting our country from outside threats? The IRS has 144,000 employees—more people than all but the 36 largest corporations in the United States. In a post-9/11 world, do we really believe we need more IRS agents than we have intelligence agents fighting the war on terror or border patrol agents on the southern and northern borders?

It is time for a reassessment and a return to reasonable taxation that spreads the responsibility, creates income, and gets government out of our lives—all without burdening our citizens. There is no way you can look at our current tax code and not see that it is trying to control every aspect of our lives. The tax code has in large part caused the growth of government and made it worse. It cannot be fixed; it must be replaced.

In addition to the $8 billion needed to operate the IRS, the cost of complying with the code amounts to at least $250 billion (that's $850 for every man, woman, and child) and is a burden to business owners large and small. That cost inhibits creativity and productivity in our workforce. Measuring, tracking, sheltering, documenting, and filing our annual income all consume a massive amount of our national wealth. The IRS is killing us, and if we are to compete, we must do away with the IRS and replace it with a National Sales Tax or what is commonly referred to as the FairTax.

As far back as Alexander Hamilton, the first secretary of the treasury, there have been discussions of a consumption tax and of why it is the best means to collect needed revenue. The founders opposed income taxes and believed such taxes would depress the economy. They may have been correct because within a generation of the beginning of the Federal income tax, America suffered the greatest economic depression in its history. As Hamilton, the first treasury secretary, said about federal taxation,

> There is no method of steering clear of this inconvenience [taxes], but by authorizing the national government to raise its own revenues in its own way. Imposts, excises, and, in general, all duties upon articles of consumption, may be compared to a fluid, which will, in time, find its level with the means of paying them. The amount to be contributed by each citizen will in a degree be at his own option, and can be regulated by an attention to his resources. The rich may be extravagant, the poor can be frugal, and private oppression may always be avoided by a judicious selection of objects proper for such impositions. If inequalities should arise in some States from duties on particular objects, these will, in all probability, be counterbalanced by proportional inequalities in other States, from the duties on other objects.
>
> . . .In the course of time and things, an equilibrium, as far as it is attainable in so complicated a subject, will be established everywhere. Or, if inequalities should still exist, they would neither be so great in their degree, so uniform in their operation, nor so odious in their appearance, as those which would necessarily spring from quotas, upon any scale that can possibly be devised. It is a single advantage of taxes on articles of consumption that they contain in their own nature a security against excess.

Alexander Hamilton made clear that a consumption tax is the only fair way to tax people. Such a tax is based on *consumption* rather than *productivity* and would allow the taxpayers to control their tax burden. We have been brainwashed into thinking the bigger the government is, the more it is doing for us. Our economy is consumption-based, so a consumption tax is the only sensible solution.

The most sensible form of consumption tax is the FairTax proposal, which will replace all federal income and payroll taxes, including personal, gift, estate, capital gains, alternative minimum, Social Security/Medicare, self-employment, and corporate taxes. The FairTax proposal ensures that no American pays federal taxes up to the poverty level, so it is progressive with the biggest consumers paying the highest rate.

To proceed with the FairTax is to repeal the 16th Amendment to the Constitution. When the FairTax is passed and goes into effect, Americans will initially pay only any state income taxes. But as the tax is implemented, I believe states will follow suit and replace their tax codes with a state sales tax. Once that occurs, Americans will keep 100 percent of their paychecks. The FairTax is revenue-neutral, will fully fund federal government spending at current levels, and will generate enough revenue to keep the promise of Social Security and Medicare. Under the FairTax, no federal income taxes or payroll taxes will be withheld from paychecks, pensions, or Social Security checks.

This country has a basic belief that we should help those who need it and that there are certain necessities that should not have to be taxed. In the FairTax proposal, there is a monthly "prebate" for every registered household to cover consumption of goods up to the poverty level. For example, if the poverty level is $20,000 for a family of four, then every family in America would receive a monthly check equal to the tax on $20,000. This would make all purchases up to the poverty level tax-free. As a result, no federal sales tax up to the poverty level will be paid, which certainly meets the "progressivity" component that many Democrats and Republicans like in today's tax system. We do believe that the tax responsibility for people making more than the poverty level is greater than for those who live at or below the poverty level. Also, resourceful people who don't mind using "pre-owned" goods could live on the prebate.

The FairTax will completely "untax" the poor, lower the tax burden on middle America, and make the overall rate progressive. What makes the FairTax progressive is that it is based on lifestyle/spending choices, rather than simply punishing those tax-payers who are successful. In other words, through our consumption choices, we decide how much tax we pay. In addition, people who are currently living outside the system and not paying their fair share of income taxes and payroll taxes will begin to contribute to the system. It is anticipated that the rate of tax would become lower once the new system settles out. Some people may argue that once the government gets our money, they will find a way to spend it rather than give it back to us. I would agree that history would support that. But what a nice problem to have—more money than we need to meet all the needs of the government and we take home our entire paycheck and have complete control of the tax we pay. Sounds pretty good to me.

In the FairTax system there will be no tax on used goods. With the FairTax we are taxed only once on any good or service. The sales tax is charged just as state sales taxes are today. Anyone who chooses to buy used goods—used cars, existing homes, used appliances—does not pay the FairTax. If business owners or farmers buy something for strictly business purposes (not for personal consump-tion), they pay no consumption tax. When we decide what to buy and how much to spend, we see exactly how much we are contribut-ing to the government with each purchase. The system is transparent and will benefit a consumption-based economy.

For the best example of how our economy has changed and, as a result, how our tax system needs to be changed, compare the after-math of the attack on Pearl Harbor in December 1941, and the attack on America on September 11, 2001. After the attack on Pearl Harbor, the government, headed by President Franklin Delano Roosevelt, encouraged people to save items, promoted the idea of planting "victory gardens" to save on food consumption, and rationed goods that might be needed for the war effort. After the

9/11 attacks on America, President Bush worried that people wouldn't go out and spend money and encouraged us to do so. We have become a consumption-based economy. We should have a tax code based on consumption.

I love to hear politicians talk about taxes on businesses. In reality, there are no such things. Currently, retail prices reflect the tax code embedded in the cost of the goods. Any taxes levied are a cost of doing business and ultimately are passed on to the consumer. One of the biggest lies is the payroll tax and the argument that the employer pays half and the employee pays half. The employee pays it all because when the employer withholds the "other side" of the payroll tax, resources to give pay raises are gone. The largest expense in most businesses is payroll, so any additional expenses and taxes will take away from the employers' ability to increase payroll. Currently, according to Dale Jorgenson, former head of the economics department at Harvard University in a study done for FairTax, 20-25 percent of the cost of goods in America is the cost of taxes and compliance with the code.

Not only does our current code hurt employers and employees, it also hampers our ability to compete in the world market. Jorgensen claims that if competition does not allow prices to rise, then corporations lower labor costs, which hurts those who can least afford to lose their jobs. Finally, if prices are as high as competition allows and labor costs are as low as is practical, then profits and dividends to shareholders are driven down. This result hurts retirement savings and pension funds invested in corporate America. The FairTax is a win-win-win tax plan where the sham of corporate taxation ends, competition drives prices down, more people in America have jobs, and retirement/pension funds see improved performance.

With all the discussion about outsourcing of jobs, it's time to accept that our tax code deters job creation and encourages outsourcing of jobs rather than products. Since the tax code is not imbedded in our manufacturing, the FairTax does not impede American exports. This gives us the ability to sell U.S. goods at a substantial reduction while maintaining similar profit margins. Lower prices will increase demand for U.S. exports, thereby increasing creation of U.S.

manufacturing jobs. It will also make American goods more affordable at home and make imported goods less attractive.

The FairTax is different from the Value Added Taxes in other countries and will again give U.S. products a definite price advantage. We forget that in the aftermath of WWII, the United States was one of the only countries with the ability to produce goods in mass quantities. Since then, Europe has rebuilt and thrived, and manufacturing has grown throughout the world. To make our goods more competitive and innovative, we have to get the imbedded tax code out of the cost of the goods and again compete on quality and price, not tax advantages.

One of the goals of the FairTax plan is to be revenue-neutral. If the FairTax is at 23 percent, replacing all federal taxes and fees, including the FICA tax, then the price of goods will go down about 25 percent. The FairTax will be added on top so the cost of consumer goods will remain neutral. This flat-rate sales tax will pay for all current government operations, including Social Security and Medicare. Government revenues are more stable and predictable than with the federal income tax because consumption is a more constant revenue base than is income. It won't be long before the FairTax will bring in so much revenue that the rate will be able to be reduced to the 17% range within five years. That will open the door to the states looking at the option of eliminating their taxes, including property tax, and joining the FairTax revolution.

For example, if you were in a 23 percent income tax bracket, the federal government would take $23 out of your paycheck for every $100 you made. With the FairTax, if the federal government gets $23 out of every $100 spent in America, the same total revenue is delivered to the federal government. This is revenue neutrality. So, instead of paycheck-earning Americans paying 15.3 percent of their paychecks in Social Security/Medicare payroll taxes, plus an average of 18 percent of their paychecks in federal income tax (for a total of about 33 percent), consumers pay only $23 out of every $100, or about 30 percent at the cash register when they purchase new goods or services for personal consumption. This tax is collected only on spending above the federal poverty level, allowing the national sales tax to be progressive.

We all know there are whole industries, operating legally and illegally, that deal in cash. We also know there is a subculture that does not comply with the IRS code. In addition, to get the "prebate" on purchases up to the family poverty level, families must have a tax ID or valid Social Security number. Illegal immigrants will have to get legal if they want to get the "prebate" on the purchases they make up to the poverty level. So, everybody, citizens or non-citizens or tourists, will contribute to the tax revenues of the United States every time they make a purchase. This will immediately allow us to collect revenues from people in this country illegally when they make purchases in the United States.

The FairTax is fair across the board. It will be easy to keep up with, will make the United States more competitive around the world, and will get the government out of our personal lives. There is no evidence to show that spending patterns would change. This is a consumption age where people are accustomed to buying everything they want. When the FairTax is passed and put into effect, there will be so much money to fund government that we will be worried our legislators will have too much money to spend.

This is the time to deal with our tax problems, and implementing the FairTax would help us with other monumental funding problems. We have to deal with all of this comprehensively, or these structures, the IRS in particular, will take away all the advantages the American economy has benefited from for the last two centuries. We have to be looking over our shoulders at the other powerful nations of the world that wish to replace us economically. The world still wants American goods, and we need to make those goods competitive again with the FairTax plan. We must ask at every opportunity of local, state, and federal elected officials who control our tax policy, "What are you doing to implement the FairTax?" The time is now.

The American
Pendulum

I have been trying to save the world for as long as I can remember. I have long had passionate points of view and I have often thought about great American issues in terms of a swinging pendulum. We push good ideas too far when we should bring them to the center, where they can be fixed and implemented.

Many ideas in American government start out great, but over time and through political maneuvering come to be unrecognizable. As a result, the issues that started the pendulum swinging never get solved. They languish and fester and harm the American people. It doesn't have to be that way. The next section will consider some hot-button issues for our nation and how both Democrats and Republicans can work to address these issues.

CHAPTER TWELVE

The War on Poverty and the Welfare State

From the wild Irish Slums of the 19th century eastern seaboard, to the riot-torn suburbs of Los Angeles, there is one unmistakable lesson in American history: A community that allows a large number of young men to grow up in broken families, dominated by women, never acquiring any stable relationship to male authority, never acquiring any rational expectations about the future—that community asks for and gets chaos.
—Senator Daniel Patrick Moynihan, (D–NY), 1965.

America never meant to create a societal dependency out of the New Deal. Programs meant to aid people with employment and which led to the creation of Social Security were meant to lift up the American people mired in the Great Depression, but our nation became side-tracked by war in the 1940s and 1950s. The 1960s only made us ready for more dependency. We can't blame anyone but ourselves for the bureaucratic monkey on our backs. We wanted to make our lives easier after the Great Depression. Our intentions were good, but they got out of control.

The irony is that the icon of the liberal Left, John F. Kennedy, was really the last conservative Democrat to lead his party, and he was the last senator to be elected from his Senate seat to the presidency. He was a tax-cutting, free-market, Communist-fighting

Democrat. He represented Americans of that time who had really never seen racism in action. Kennedy didn't truly believe it until there were glimpses of it on the campaign trail and then savagely on our television screens. He was a reluctant warrior on the civil rights stage and, like most of America, was convinced of the need for change by the images of the early 1960s. Kennedy thought he was the beginning of an era, the first president, "born in this century, tempered by war, disciplined by a hard and bitter peace, proud of our ancient heritage—and unwilling to witness or permit the slow undoing of those human rights to which this nation has always been committed, and to which we are committed today at home and around the world."

These eloquent words from Kennedy's inaugural address meant to signal a new beginning but in reality eulogized the end of the era of Democrats who were valued for their stands on both military and social issues. Our national innocence ended with the death of President Kennedy and then the failure of the Johnson presidency. It was during this time that we began to link, in our collective American consciousness, rights for all people and the responsibility of government to provide these rights.

It was during this time that Americans finally looked in the mirror and understood the problems we had with poverty. The difference between the New Deal of FDR and the Great Society of LBJ, however, is that Roosevelt tried to lift up *all* poverty and Johnson, overtaken with the Civil Rights movement, focused simply on urban poverty. While attempting to end poverty was (and *is*) a noble goal, we focus too much on urban poverty and too little on rural poverty.

President Kennedy pushed for the passage of Civil Rights legislation during the summer and fall before his death. After President Kennedy's assassination, President Johnson made the passage of these bills his first priority. With Republican and Democratic support, the bills were passed and signed into law. The passage of these bills is one of the great achievements of this republic because they represent our ability to identify a societal problem, draft and pass legislation to address it, and implement the law for the national good. (Notice that there are no courts in this equation.)

But then President Johnson unveiled the Great Society. It was supposed to change the world and end poverty, but it actually made things worse. If you *give* people what you think are the keys out of poverty and they lack the education and opportunity to keep those keys, they will fail. The Great Society was based on opportunity without preparation or expectation. You have to create opportunity and remove barriers. The pendulum effect stipulates that the failure of these systems to lift people out of poverty was a result of optimistic planning by policymakers who believed American economic growth would make possible bold new public efforts. It was a noble goal, and had the original plans been left to develop on their own, I believe the process would have been more successful.

But as the Great Society proposals developed, there were knee-jerk reactions to rising social strife and violence in the African-American struggle for equality. Rather than removing the barriers and providing opportunity, government tried to guarantee the outcome. Additionally, liberal Democrats in the majority at that time were married to the conviction that only a "public effort" (federal tax dollars) could eliminate poverty and prevent social disorder. This was when the Left began trying to homogenize the faith movement to create a moral relativism that said a bureaucracy was as effective as a faith-based group in helping impoverished people. However, by "poverty" Democrats meant *urban* poverty rather than *all* poverty. They always play to their base. Poverty is poverty. Poor whites with little education or opportunity encounter the same obstacles as poor blacks with little education and opportunity. The debate over affirmative action would be over if we would make it colorblind and accept that poor people of any color need a little help from government and wealthy people of any color need government to get out of the way. Education and opportunity and culture—not race—separate us.

The climate for the Great Society was created by the passing of the 1964 Civil Rights Act, which addressed job discrimination and the segregation of public accommodations, as well as the 1965 Voting Rights Act, which guaranteed black voting rights. In 1968, housing discrimination was addressed, and constitutional protections to Native Americans on reservations were extended. With the great beginning of these laws, a large drain on our tax base came through welfare payments to people in poverty.

When Daniel Patrick Moynihan's mother was on "aid to widows and children," she had been abandoned by her husband and went back to school so she could support her family. This was what welfare was supposed to be—temporary help for people, especially women and children, who have fallen on hard times. That is what it was for many years. That same Daniel Patrick Moynihan worked for the Department of Labor in the Johnson administration and later became a great senator and statesman from New York.

In March 1965, before Daniel Patrick Moynihan was a senator and while he worked for the Department of Labor, he published a report, "The Negro Family, A Case for National Action," from the Office of Policy Planning and Research in the United States Department of Labor. It disclosed that in the 1950s, when unemployment went down, poverty rates went down among African Americans. But through the 1960s, the study showed poverty rates continued to rise regardless of the status of unemployment. He concluded that the breakdown of the family was in part being caused by the welfare system and that the stable family is an integral part of financial stability. In early 2005, Martha Stewart was released from prison in West Virginia and had this to say upon her release: "I can tell you now that I feel very fortunate to have had a family that nurtured me, the advantage of an excellent education, and the opportunity to pursue the American dream." These are exactly the points that Moynihan was trying to make in 1965—it takes a stable and supportive family, as well as opportunity for education and employment, to pursue the American dream. As with Medicare, we knew the welfare system was not working soon after we created it. The government could have fixed the problems early in the process before we created generations of people dependent on welfare.

The pendulum was pushed in 1965 when the government knew that, regardless of the economy, whether unemployment rates were up or down, the welfare system was costing more and more with no better results for the recipients. Yet the government allowed

Americans to continue to participate in a broken program for more than thirty years after that. How many generations of the underprivileged were imprisoned by a promise that couldn't be kept? As I'll discuss later in this book, our elected officials are guilty of the same offense with the Medicare system.

Since it doesn't have to be that way, then what do we do? First of all, when it comes to the poor and government programs, no one should get something for nothing. The Welfare Reform Act of the late 1990s began the process of reform. The key to any government program is that those who benefit from the taxpayer dollars used to pay for the program should be required to give something in return. We saw from the Great Society that in some of our best economic times, people in poverty did no better. A rising tide can lift all boats only if everyone has a boat in the water. If you're on the shore, you're still stuck.

We must also require that people who are supported by the state be high school graduates. We require people on welfare or receiving food stamps to be high school graduates or enrolled in a GED program if they are more than eighteen-years-old. We should also require any state or federal inmate who doesn't have a high school diploma to get a GED as a requirement for release. We must discontinue the attitude of "poor people can't." They *can* if they are going to receive government services at the expense of the taxpayers. There are no government services without the taxpayers, so the taxpayers are in charge and their interests come first.

I have always had a problem with the term "poor." In the paragraphs above we are talking about material *and* cultural poverty. America made a serious mistake in thinking we could fix cultural or social ills with money. It is a serious mistake to think that money without responsibility or expectations will solve anyone's problems. In one of my first interviews, I spoke with John Stossel about his special, "The Mystery of Happiness." Stossel found that money will make people happier to the extent that it supplies basic needs such as shelter, food, clothing, and mobility. After that, people must have the opportunity to earn what they have. If they don't, there is an emptiness that must be filled. Many times it is filled with the wrong things.

Many of the poor in America own homes, cars, and jewelry, and have services like cable TV and cell phones. Very few of us are poor by the world's standards. So what is the government's role in fighting poverty? Its role is to provide a *temporary* safety net. Getting the government out of their lives is the best way to get the poor out of poverty. Use any government service to get an education and think about what you can do to make your life better without government help. Bring the pendulum back to the center on this issue.

CHAPTER THIRTEEN

Social Security

In the important field of security for our old people, it seems necessary to adopt three principles: First, non-contributory old-age pensions for those who are now too old to build up their own insurance. It is, of course, clear that for perhaps thirty years to come funds will have to be provided by the States and the Federal Government to meet these pensions. Second, compulsory contributory annuities that in time will establish a self-supporting system for those now young and for future generations. Third, voluntary contributory annuities by which individual initiative can increase the annual amounts received in old age. It is proposed that the Federal Government assume one-half of the cost of the old-age pension plan, which ought ultimately to be supplanted by self-supporting annuity plans.
—Franklin Delano Roosevelt, President of the United States, to a
Joint Session of Congress, January 17, 1935

The first item I ever had published was a letter to the editor about Franklin Delano Roosevelt. While he is a liberal icon for Democrats, when you look at his words and his actions, he was fiscally conservative. Granted, in a presidency spanning thirteen years, the longest ever, you could probably find a pattern of behavior to suit any point of view. All the programs he instituted were intended to be temporary or eventually self-sustaining. One wonders what FDR would think if he could analyze the discussion of Social Security today.

Social Security was a great idea that has morphed into a program that doesn't do what we need it to do. At the time of its signing, FDR said,

> We can never insure 100 percent of the population against 100 percent of the hazards and vicissitudes of life. But we have tried to frame a law which will give some measure of protection to the average citizen and to his family against the loss of a job and against poverty-ridden old age. This law, too, represents a cornerstone in a structure which is being built, but is by no means complete . . . . It is . . . a law that will take care of human needs and at the same time provide for the United States an economic structure of vastly greater soundness.

By 1961, during the first months of his administration, President Kennedy said, "the Social Security program plays an important part in providing for families, children, and older persons in times of stress. But it cannot remain static. Changes in our population, in our working habits, and in our standard of living require constant revision." Two things are apparent from this statement. One is that, even by the 1960s, Social Security had become an expectation by the public. The other is that, with the money rolling in, the program had been expanded far beyond its original form. Can you see the pendulum swinging?

The facts today are that Social Security will have to reduce benefits or it will have to restructure. If we do nothing to the structure of the system, benefits will be reduced 25 percent by 2042. It is true that as long as there are workers there will always be money in the Social Security plan. But what will it be able to pay?

There is much discussion about whether Social Security is in a crisis or not. It depends on the definition. We know people who are beginning their careers now are going to need a different kind of Social Security, and it is the responsibility of this administration to fix it. By the time these young workers are old enough to hold the offices that legislators and the president have today, their choices will be severely limited. It is the responsibility of the elected officials to deal with this problem. All they need to know to make the case for change is that sixteen workers supported one retiree in 1950, while three workers support one retiree today.

It doesn't take a Nobel Prize-winning economist to see the direction Social Security is going. If this group of legislators won't act, then history will look at them as the ones who destroyed the hopes and dreams of the young workers of this young century. That is not a threat; it is a promise.

It is clear to many people that something needs to be done, but for some reason the Democratic Party is afraid of people building wealth and self-reliance. When Daniel Patrick Moynihan was asked why Democrats were so dead set on not changing Social Security (after they were in favor of it in the Clinton administration), he said, "It's because they worry that wealth will turn Democrats into Republicans."

Much has been made by the Democrats regarding a statement from President Bush at the March 16, 2005, press conference. He was asked about his plan for Social Security. He pointed out that he had purposely not laid out a detailed plan because he wanted everything to be on the table. He wants to get away from the "microphone mentality" that lawmakers are in now. They go to the microphone instead of to the worktable to solve our national problems. The president said to the press in attendance, "Personal accounts do not solve the issue. But personal accounts will make sure that individual workers get a better deal with whatever emerges as a Social Security solution." The Democratic National Committee took about a week to pounce, but pounce they did. In absence of a plan, the DNC criticized and continues to criticize the president.

Regardless of Democratic inaction, the fact is that there will be benefit cuts or there will be big tax increases. In light of the benefit cuts, the best thing to do is to add private accounts to the system and then offer a reduced fixed benefit and a private account on top. In every cycle since the Great Depression, investments have earned more than Social Security benefits pay. Wealth will set people free, and we should allow people to leave their private account inheritance to their families or designated beneficiaries.

We know private accounts work. We have examples in countries like Chile and even in our own country. In the early days of Social Security, some groups were allowed to opt out. In every system that opted out, the benefits far exceeded the Social Security benefits in every way. They don't like to talk about it, but ask retired teachers in your area or government employees. Many of them participated in programs that opted out of the Social Security system, and they are doing very well. Americans need to move their legislators to the table and tell them they want a retirement plan—not a welfare plan. They should say that they want a chance to build wealth. But this still will not be the whole answer.

Until the early 1980s, certain groups could opt out of Social Security if they provided a plan on their own. Mostly included were state and local governments and school systems. Galveston County in Texas was one of those places that opted out. In 2002, I interviewed Judge Ray Holbrook, who was a Galveston County judge from 1967 to 1995 and who oversaw the creation and administration of the Galveston County alternative plan. In 1980, Galveston County workers were offered a retirement alternative to Social Security. As expected, some were interested and others were fearful of the loss of security. Judge Holbrook said, "After twenty-one years, folks here can say they are doing two to four times better than what they would have gotten from Social Security." Recently, in an article for *USA Today*, Judge Holbrook restated, "after twenty-four years, folks here can say unequivocally that when Galveston County pulled out of the Social Security system in 1981, we were on the road to providing our workers with a better deal than Franklin Roosevelt's New Deal." Galveston County began looking at alternative plans in 1979, when many of the same concerns arose about Social Security's solvency in the long run. The goal, according to Judge Holbrook, was to provide the same or better benefits, with no tax increases or risk. The county also wanted to have a benefit that could be passed on to family members upon death.

The plan was called a "banking model" rather than an "investment model." Since one of the goals was no risk, the workers put their contributions into conservative fixed-rate annuities. The result is an average of a 6.5 percent annual rate of return over the last twenty-four years as updated since I discussed this with Judge Holbrook in 2002. Galveston County has been able to provide greatly increased benefits in survivorship and disability.

Here's how the Galveston County workers compare in benefits to the Social Security System:

- •Workers making $17,000 a year are expected to receive about 50 percent more per month on our alternative plan than on Social Security—$1,036 instead of $683.
- • Workers making $26,000 a year will make almost double Social Security, $1,500 instead of $853.
- • Workers making $51,000 a year will get $3,103 instead of $1,368.
- • Workers making $75,000 or more will nearly triple Social Security, $4,540 instead of $1,645.
- • Survivorship benefits pay four times a worker's annual salary—a minimum of $75,000 to a maximum $215,000—rather than Social Security's customary onetime $255 survivorship to a spouse (with no minor children). If the worker dies before retirement, the survivors receive not only the full survivorship but get generous accidental death benefits too.
- • Disability benefit pays 60 percent of an individual's salary, better than Social Security's.

The original Galveston plan was not perfect and was adjusted over time. Until January 2005, workers were allowed to make hardship withdrawals that affected their long-term gains. The important thing is that this program works and could be a model for the rest of the country. One of the recommendations Judge Holbrook made (and with which I concur) is that the participation in the privatization plan should be voluntary at first and slowly phased into mandatory participation. The Galveston County plan proved that low-income workers would do better, but we should debate a guarantee of benefits for lower income levels. Judge Holbrook said in that same *USA Today* article,

Our experience should be judged factually and fairly, not emotionally, politically, or on the basis of hearsay. We sought a secure,
risk-free alternative to the Social Security system, and it has
worked very well for nearly a quarter-century. Our retirees have
prospered, and our working people have had the security of generous disability and accidental death benefits. Most important, we
didn't force our children and grandchildren to be unduly taxed and
burdened for our retirement care while these fine young people are
struggling to raise and provide for their own families. What has
been good for Galveston County may, indeed, be good for this
country.

We know the answer to this problem and we have a strong, safe,
and proven system in the Galveston County model on which to base
the federal program. Let's not waste any more time. Social Security at
its beginning was a "liberal idea with conservative implementation,"
as David Walker, Comptroller General of the United States, said,
because life was physically hard and people didn't live long much
beyond 65 years if they lived that long. Today, if you live to be 65
and are healthy, you will live to be 80 on average. A baby born today,
especially if female, could live to be 100 years old. It is time to fix the
system, but the system is not the whole answer.

We all need to live more like our grandparents and great-grandparents did. We should save from every paycheck, be able to separate
needs from wants and luxuries from necessities. Finish school. Pay
yourself first. Stay out of debt. Don't finance a car for more than two
years or a house for more than fifteen years. Do these things and you
will live well no matter what the government does. And if you do all
that, Social Security, if it is still around, will be nothing more than a
nice retirement bonus.

CHAPTER FOURTEEN

Public Education

If the only motive was to help people who could not afford education, advocates of government involvement would have simply proposed tuition subsidies.
—Milton Friedman, 1976 Nobel Prize winner in economics

The biggest problem in public education today is that parents have forgotten that education is not an entitlement. Rather, it is a privilege to attend school. Parents expect to be able to drop their children off for pre-K and pick them up as educated adults after twelfth grade. Many parents have abdicated their responsibilities to continue education at home. After-school time is not free time for plopping our children down in front of the television for the evening. There has to be interaction between parents and children on books and literature, world history and current events. Parents should be practicing life skills with their children and teaching them to be adults. Schools run by the government cannot raise our children, nor should we want them to.

I do take issue with some of my colleagues who use the term "government schools" with disdain. The fact of the matter is there are very good public schools and there are very bad public schools. The difference is not money; it is parental involvement. If parents, students, and especially elected officials don't start to look at public school as a gift rather than an entitlement, we will lose the educational battle in this country.

By and large, politicians give lip service to education. I mean, who wouldn't be in favor of children being educated? "It's for the children" is their mantra. But beyond that? I just don't see it. My husband and I are the products of public education, and my children have been educated in public schools and so far have gone to public colleges. There are other debates we will have on other issues, but parents are the ingredient public schools need. It has to be "old school," where the parents support teachers who are there to teach. As the schools have become more administrative and the teachers have been separated from the process, the education process has become tougher.

The Importance of Local Control

Government has not helped education in America. The more layers of national bureaucracy there are, the worse our educational systems get. Only at the local school level, where qualified leaders can make decisions with the interests of children at heart, can real educational reform take place. It is for this reason that I advocate the elimination of the federal Department of Education. I also believe most state departments of education should be eliminated. The old saying is, "lead, follow, or get out of the way." Departments of education should lead with proven strategies, follow schools and systems that work, or go away and let teachers teach. I believe in local control. There is no better determiner of what is best for a group of students than the local school system or the local school board.

One of the obstacles to local control is that of old civil rights leaders, who are mostly Democrats, believing that if local control is returned to school districts, we will return to the days of segregation. This attitude is preposterous. Now that the barrier of segregation has been removed, schools should be competitive and independent. I know it is radical, but incremental improvement hasn't worked. We must look at what *does* work and enable schools to adopt policies that work for them. The opportunity for an education is a gift from the taxpayers to all school-age children who live in this country. That gift includes the teachers, administrators, buildings, etc. We all benefit from good public schools, and it is the responsibility of parents and children to maximize those educational opportunities.

"Town Tuitioning"

There is an example of this greater local control in the Vermont and Maine school systems. Since the mid 1800s, Vermont and Maine have practiced "town tuitioning," in which intergovernmental vouchers give parents choice in education. In 2002, Christopher Hammons extensively studied this system. In his study, titled "The Effects of Town Tuitioning in Vermont and Maine," he concluded that if students are thought of as customers of education, rather than as wards of the state, there would be an effect on the suppliers of education. School choice contends that competition for students, not governments, would improve schools and attract more money for education. Maine and Vermont provide the best opportunity to look at the issue of school choice and better education delivery.

Christopher Hammons finds that the impetus for the "town tuitioning" system in Maine and Vermont came about because of children living in rural and non-urban areas. The system allows parents living in districts that do not own and operate elementary or secondary schools to send their children to public or nonsectarian private schools in other areas of the state—or even outside the state—using funds provided by the child's home district. Most districts can provide good elementary schools, but it becomes more difficult to provide the rigorous curriculum for middle school and high school, so there are many more high school students than elementary school students taking advantage of tuitioning. This system has been in effect since 1869 in Vermont and since 1873 in Maine, meaning that these voucher programs have existed in the United States for more than 100 years and are adapted to reflect local needs.

Hammons concluded three things in his study. First, he recognized that schools perform better in a choice environment because choice provides a strong incentive and desire to improve performance to attract more students (and with them, valuable tuition dollars). Schools in Maine and Vermont with higher standardized test scores attract more tuition money from parents. The relationship between tuition money and test scores was compelling evidence that schools are willing to work harder when competing with each other for tuition dollars. Test scores in Vermont and Maine were higher in places of higher concentrations of tuition towns and high schools. That is, test scores were higher in areas with the greatest possible competition and lower in areas with little or no competition for tuition dollars.

Second, Hammons identified that the benefits of the system spread across all demographic groups. In fairness, there is not much racial diversity in Maine and Vermont (both states are over 95 percent white), but there is economic diversity. Tuition towns—those that allow tuitioning—have higher standardized test scores than non-tuition schools, whether affluent or poor, rural or urban. The study concluded that if school choice is expanded to towns that do not currently have it, more tuition dollars will be attracted and, based on history, achievement should improve.

Finally, Hammons found that the benefit to these schools went beyond school performance. Competition not only attracted more money to the school systems but also, over time, reduced the spending per pupil by almost $1,000. This program provides substantial economic benefit to both states with minimal costs and provides a greater return on current education spending. African Americans support the concept of vouchers at a rate of well over 50 percent, and most conservatives and Republicans support the concept of vouchers. The sad truth is that a few members are trying to block the will of the people in Congress, and the people are letting these members have a pass on this instead of demanding a change. This is a grassroots effort that people can win if they put their time and resources behind the change.

A Changing Workplace

Education is the key to success, and it is the single most important thing parents do for children. Many parents dream of college and great lives for their children. It is clear that post-secondary education is a necessity in this and future economies. At the same time, the percentage of jobs requiring a four-year college education has remained the same over the last twenty-five years.

What *has* changed is the number of skilled and technical jobs. In rough numbers, according to the U.S. Department of Labor and the Bureau of Labor Statistics, 22 percent of jobs require a four-year degree—a number that has remained fairly static over the last twenty-five years. Within that 22 percent there are jobs that are in short supply, but overall the number of jobs requiring a college degree hovers in the low 20 percent range. Of the remaining 80 percent of jobs, about 15 percent of jobs used to be technical and about 85 percent used to be unskilled or jobs with on-site training. Today, about 85 percent are technical and 15 percent are unskilled. It is essential that every student completes high school and finishes at least two years of post-secondary education to be competitive in this job market.

But education reform won't happen on its own and it won't happen at the hands of the federal government. In order to stop the pendulum swing in America on education, several things have to happen. First, parents have to be involved—not just in school but at home too. Education happens at home and at school. We have to have school choice and get the money, the administration, and the school as close together as possible. Parents must insist that their children finish high school and be proactive in helping their children choose a post-secondary option, whether that choice is technical school, community college, university, or the military.

President Bush talked about the "soft bigotry of low expectations" in education. He was primarily talking about minority students, but I would argue that we should not have low expectations of our schools. If schools don't help students achieve, then parents should have the opportunity to send their children to a better school.

If we are to expect our children to finish their education with the support of their parents and community, then we must allow room for school choice. That is the American way.

It is a privilege for the children of this country that the taxpayers spend so much of their money on public education, and we must treat the taxpayers with respect and earn the education offered. Teachers and administrators cannot give children an education; children must want it. Education is a responsibility of parents from the day the child is born to the day the child supports himself or herself. Everyone benefits from a well-educated child, but the answer to education is not more money. The answer to education is that parents and children view it as a gift and the government offers a choice and creates competition in education with the goal of excellence from the school and the student. Nothing less should be expected.

CHAPTER FIFTEEN

The Courts

The lesson is, in a truly democratic society—or at least the one in America—one way or another people will have their say on significant social policy. . . . If judges are routinely providing the society's definitive answers to moral questions on which there is ample room for debate . . . then judges will be made politically accountable.
—Antonin Scalia, Supreme Court Justice of
the United States of America

History is filled with the examples of the government pushing the pendulum from one end of the political spectrum to the other. When the Supreme Court decided *Plessy v. Ferguson*, which established the concept of "separate but equal," it was a case of the court going too far. The Constitution says nothing about "separate but equal." Instead, the Constitution clearly states that there should be "equal access" under the law. When *Brown v. Board of Education* came along years later, it partially fixed the problem. It overturned *Plessy v. Ferguson*, and it began the long road to desegregation. But anytime a change is forced, there are unintended consequences.

When *Brown v. Board of Education* was decided, the state and federal governments interpreted it as mandatory integration. The implementation led to busing and the upheaval of many students, black and white. It was actually many years until the integration of Southern schools was complete. The result of forced integration was the loss of the jobs of many African-American teachers and the loss of the sense of community that schools in African-American neighborhoods provided. Many accomplishments of that time and place were lost; many community role models lost authority positions, and everyone lost their neighborhood schools. In turn, this loss of community instituted by the social results of *Brown v. Board of Education* contributed to the breakdown of the family, to "white flight" to the suburbs, and to a resegregation of schools—not by race, but by geography. *Brown v. Board of Education* is one of the greatest decisions the Supreme Court has made because it fixed an egregious error in the findings of Plessy, but its interpretation was incorrect because it resulted in forced integration.

There was so much controversy throughout the South on how to implement the decision of *Brown v. Board of Education* that many schools did not integrate until the early 1970s. In the Gainesville City Schools in Hall County, Georgia, for instance, there had always been African-American members of the school board, even during segregation. So integration went smoothly there, though a consequence was that the largely African-American Butler High School was closed and there was a great loss in that community of history and experience.

When my mother, Juanita Mitchell, was active in the PTA for the school in Muscogee County, Georgia, where my older siblings attended, she suggested a system that would first integrate kindergarten and then the next year integrate kindergarten and first grade, and so on until the schools were integrated through the twelfth grade. I have always believed that her plan of gradual integration would have worked. As it happened, it took until 1972 for Georgia schools to completely desegregate—sixteen years after my mother made her recommendation.

In DeKalb County, Georgia, where I attended school, integration was complete in 1972 with the institution of the "M and M" rule. This rule allowed children who were in the majority in one school to go to another school where they were in the minority. I attended Columbia High School, which was a new school with more than 2000 students. In 1972, less than 10 percent of the students were black. By 1977, less than 20 percent of the students were white. Forced integration, caused by the misinterpretation of *Brown v. Board of Education*, led to white flight to the suburbs.

I believe the actual intent of the court decision was to lift the barriers to integration and allow integration to happen. The unintended consequences were that many good black schools were closed and many good black teachers were left out of the loop in the new schools. The interpretation of this ruling eliminated the opportunity for many educated black men and women to be role models in their own community—a blow to the community and to the families of those neighborhoods.

But the pendulum has come back on this issue. People under forty have vastly different attitudes about race than many people over sixty. Equal opportunity is the law of the land and has been for two generations now. There is no other issue that highlights more brightly the beauty of the Constitution and the founders who wrote it. It proves the document lives on without the need to make it "living." The founders had very different personal views on race than people of today, but inherently they knew all men are created equal and they provided in the Constitution the tools for the law to support that, even if they were not ready to face it at the time.

An integrated society is essential for the optimum opportunity to be realized. The opportunity must be taken. It cannot be given; a person must work for it. In my entire life, I have never seen a person who is willing to work be unsuccessful in America. We are better for our struggles, not worse. At the time of *Brown v. Board of Education*, it would have been unimaginable for an African American like Colin Powell or Condoleezza Rice to become secretary of state. It would have been unimaginable that the face the United States would show to the world as the face of diplomacy would be one of color. We have come a very long way.

"Equal access" is what was required by the Supreme Court decision of *Brown v. Board of Education*, not the decimation of the entire social structure of the African-American middle and working class in America. We are still reeling from that decision, though many good things came from it. My children cannot imagine a school that would not accept people of color. The stigma of interracial relationships has largely been removed and the barriers we now face are economic and educational.

The Supreme Court has been filled with flawed men and women who forgot what their purpose was. In this republic it is our responsibility, if we want to change things, to convince our fellow citizens of our point of view and seek legislation to conform to that view. The courts should not be the last word on policy. They should only deal with the Constitution and what it says.

Antonin Scalia is the voice of the Constitution movement for the courts. As Scalia is vilified today by the Left as being out of the mainstream, one must remember he was confirmed with a vote of 98–0. Many of the same senators who call him "out of the mainstream" voted for him. If you look at his record, it is the senators who have changed, not Scalia. Antonin Scalia is a believer in the Constitution. It is not a living document in his eye; in fact, he has said that he is the defender of a dead Constitution—and I am too. The mainstream, mostly liberal media cannot stand this—that Justice Scalia actually stands for something and is unwilling to back down to their pressures. These are the members of the media who voted at a rate of 87 percent for Bill Clinton. Bill Clinton never received a majority in either of his elections to president, but the liberal media believes Clinton was a man of the people—their people. Antonin Scalia is a hero as protector of the foundation of our republic. As many great heroes of a noble cause, he has to take the arrows, and he does it well and with a sense of humor.

We don't need to fix the Constitution; we need to follow it. We must solve the judicial crisis of activist courts. The role of the courts is to interpret legislation, not to create policy. It is the role of Americans to convince enough of their fellow Americans to convince their legislators to pass legislation they believe in. It is the role of the courts to come into play only in making sure that legislation is constitutional. When the Massachusetts Supreme Court said the Massachusetts legislature had one year to make same-sex marriages legal, they were in fact *creating* legislation, not *interpreting* it. They all should have been impeached and removed from the court.

In a recent discussion on C-Span, Justice Scalia said,

If you think aficionados of a living Constitution want to bring you
flexibility, think again. You think the death penalty is a good idea,
fine. Persuade your fellow citizens to adopt it. You want a right to
abortion? Persuade your fellow citizens and enact it. That's flexibility. When a court rules one way or the other on something, you
lose all flexibility, particularly when its matters have nothing to do
with the law. . . .

Unelected justices too often choose to read new rights into the
Constitution at the expense of the democratic process. Look at
abortion. It's off the democratic stage. Prohibiting abortion is
unconstitutional, now and forever, coast to coast until I guess we
amend the Constitution.

It is time to get back to what the courts are supposed to be: a co-
equal branch of government, one that you seek the counsel of after
you have gone through the legislative and executive branch steps.
The courts are not meant to be makers of law. They are not meant to
be definers of society. They are not meant to be leaders of our great
nation. They are protectors of the rule of law, guardians of the sacred
trust of our Constitution. In our courts, the pendulum should never
topple the scales of Lady Justice.

CHAPTER SIXTEEN

Religious Freedom

And can the liberties of a nation be thought secure when we have removed their only firm basis, a conviction in the minds of the people that these liberties are the gift of God? That they are not to be violated but with his wrath? Indeed I tremble for my country when I reflect that God is just: that his justice cannot sleep for ever.
—Thomas Jefferson, Notes on the State of Virginia,
January 18, 1781

The First Amendment of the Constitution says, "Congress shall make no law respecting an establishment of religion, or prohibiting the free exercise thereof; or abridging the freedom of speech, or of the press; or the right of the people peaceably to assemble, and to petition the government for a redress of grievances." All of the arguments made in the opening chapters of this book pertain to this issue. The founders believed in God and they believed all that was given to the infant United States of America was given by God. There was no question for the founders that the church and the state could never be separated. The very nation itself came to us from God.

About forty years ago, the discussion began to go off track. There were decisions made by the Supreme Court that expanded the definition of "Congress" in the First Amendment to mean any public building, which is clearly not what was intended by the founders. In fact, the founders expected some states would have their own religion. Then there were a flurry of decisions that had no consistency, and the Supreme Court basically said they will take each case individually. What we are left with is a patchwork of decisions without rhyme or reason. In the quote that opens the chapter, Thomas Jefferson makes the argument that will settle all arguments across this country on religious symbols or the invoking of God in the public square: the viewing of a symbol or the hearing of the name of God does not establish a religion. As Thomas Jefferson wrote, ". . . it does me no injury for my neighbor to say there are twenty gods or no god. It neither picks my pocket, nor breaks my leg." The mere sight of a religious symbol is neither religion itself nor the establishment of religion.

In Newt Gingrich's book *Winning the Future*, the former senator mentions there are walking tours of Washington, DC, that guide visitors to all the places where God is mentioned on buildings and in public places throughout the city. It is ironic that the Supreme Court is convened in a building covered with religious symbols and yet they rule on issues of religious symbols in America.

The pendulum of the challenging of religious symbols in the public square will someday spill over to the historic symbols of this republic we cherish so much. It is important that we treat these symbols with the reverence they deserve or else when we decide to contest the elimination of religious symbols from public view, we will have degraded their meaning so much that we will not be able to win the battle to restore these symbols to the public square.

A contemporary example of this is the battle of the display of Confederate monuments and the use of the Confederate battle flag on state flags or on government property. During and after Reconstruction, many whites looked the other way when the Ku Klux Klan wrapped themselves in the "Stars and Bars" and used the flag to intimidate racial and religious minorities. By their silence, the white majority allowed the symbol to be degraded. By the time the Sons of Confederate Veterans took the Klan to court to stop using the battle flag in 1981, the damage was done. It had become a symbol of hate, not because of the men who died under it, but because of people who disrespected the dead by allowing white supremacists to misuse the flag. The Confederate battle flag will never have the meaning it once had because of its misuse more than 100 years after the Civil War—not because it flew during the Civil War. In respect for symbols of the Confederacy or symbols of the religious beliefs we hold, we must be vigilant in protecting them or we will lose the right to use them altogether.

Another example of the debate is the use of the words "under God" in the Pledge of Allegiance. Saying the words does not establish a religion. One of the best examples of explaining what the Pledge of Allegiance means came from the comedian Red Skelton during the January 14, 1969, airing of the *Red Skelton Show*, and I can't say it any better:

> I've been listening to you boys and girls recite the Pledge of Allegiance all semester and it seems as though it is becoming monotonous to you. If I may, may I recite it and try to explain to you the meaning of each word?
>
> *~I~*
> me, an individual, a committee of one.
>
> *~Pledge~*
> dedicate all of my worldly goods to give without self-pity.
>
> *~ Allegiance~*
> my love and my devotion.
>
> *~To the flag~*
> our standard, Old Glory, a symbol of freedom. Wherever she waves, there's respect because your loyalty has given her a dignity that shouts freedom is everybody's job!
>
> *~United ~*
> that means that we have all come together.
>
> *~States~*
> individual communities that have united into forty-eight great states. Forty-eight individual communities with pride and dignity and purpose; all divided with imaginary boundaries, yet united to a common purpose, and that's love for country.
>
> *~And to the republic~*
> a state in which sovereign power is invested in representatives chosen by the people to govern. And government is the people

and it's from the people to the leaders, not from the leaders to the people.

   ~For which it stands, one nation~
one nation, meaning "so blessed by God"

   ~Indivisible~
incapable of being divided.

   ~With liberty~
which is freedom; the right of power to live one's own life without threats, fear or some sort of retaliation.

   ~And Justice~
the principle or quality of dealing fairly with others.

   ~For all~
which means, boys and girls, it's as much your country as it is mine.

   Since I was a small boy, two states have been added to our country and two words have been added to the Pledge of Allegiance . . . UNDER GOD. Wouldn't it be a pity if someone said that is a prayer and that would be eliminated from schools too?

   I play the audio of the above quote on *The Martha Zoller Show* every chance I get, especially on holidays. I get such a response because it is elegant and reasonable and right. Religious freedom is something we must fight for every day. The other side is fighting to take it away from us. I use the word *evil* sparingly in my life. I was brought up to believe that the worst thing you could say about something was that it was evil, but the evil thing about the other side of this issue is it is those who have no real religious faith who want to wipe out any expression of faith in this country. The mere mention of God is offensive to them. This sensitivity is ridiculous at best and evil at worst. Our founders knew the very existence of the colonies was an opportunity from God to make something good out of a world that had seemed to go bad.

   In 1765, John Adams wrote extensively on this and believed America to be "the opening grand scene and design in Providence for the illumination of the ignorant and the emancipation of the slavish part of mankind all over the earth." He had high expectations that came from God and he knew Americans had to be able to listen to divine providence. America is built on and thrives on this providence of God and on the free expression of religion, not the repression of religion. The conservative movement of the last decade bears witness to the swinging of the pendulum back to its proper place in relation to how Americans view the open expression of their religious heritage. We are getting back on track in this country in what I believe to be the beginning of another Great Awakening in our nation's history.

At the Dawn of a New Great Awakening

I have been accused throughout my life of being too positive and looking at life through rose-colored glasses. I admit that is true. I believe in America and her principles, and I believe in her basic goodness. I also believe most Americans feel this way. We make mistakes, but as Gordon Sinclair said, we learn from those mistakes and we are optimistic. Further, we uncover, examine, and debate those mistakes openly.

Around the world, people wonder why America appears so united, so incredibly single-minded on most big issues. There is no doubt we are at the dawn of a new Great Awakening in this country. "Great Awakenings" are times when strong religious beliefs mix with politics and cause things to change, both in government and often in organized churches. Historians say there have been three "Great Awakenings" in United States history, each lasting fifty to one hundred years, and each happening at a time of great change in lifestyle across the country.

The first "Great Awakening" began about 1730 and, according to Robert William Fogel, author of *The Fourth Great Awakening and the Future of Egalitarianism* and winner of the 1993 Nobel Prize in Economics, ". . . ripened into the American Revolution against the British Crown." The second began about 1800 and ". . . produced the crusade against slavery that eventuated in the Civil War." The third "Great Awakening" began about 1900 and is more complicated as society had changed from agrarian to industrial, from rural to urban, and as modernists and "Social Gospelers" had laid the political foundation for the welfare state. Great things are accomplished during these times and I look with anticipation to the future in this great nation.

The ideals set out by this nation and its Constitution are lofty and should be reached for at all costs. We see that in the sacrifices of our soldiers every day. But what is just as important is the daily lives of people who lead this country according to a shared sense of values. Americans are not only united by the land and history of success in the world, but by the shared bond of freedom to be the people the Creator made us to be has worked the miracle that is America.

While the liberal media likes to make Americans seem divided over this political squabble or that, overall, Americans believe in the cause of America. Americans do not work well with cynicism; it is the single thing that can undermine us. The Left has already given up. They don't believe in the kind of country that the rest of us believe in. They believe the worst in America, not the best. It is that attitude that must be fought with words and with actions by holding our leaders accountable to the values we share.

But most of all, this cynical attitude must be fought by simply continuing to live the lives of impenetrable conviction that have made us the strongest nation in the history of the world, that have made us to this day what Puritan John Winthrop called a "city upon a hill." That dream is what makes our republic work. It is what makes us, the great American nation, truly *indivisible*.

INDEX

Biography

Martha Zoller is a force in the talk radio world today. As a child, the youngest of four children, the family dinner table was always filled with discussions of current events. Those discussions led to her passion for politics, while her experiences as an adult have led her to conservative values.

After graduating in 1979 from the University of Georgia with a degree in journalism, Martha worked in the corporate world, while also becoming a wife, mother, and stepmother. She has stayed at home and juggled children and working priorities. Martha Zoller knows there is no glass ceiling and that women can have it all, just not at the same time.

Martha began her talk radio career in 1994 after being a regular caller to WDUN AM 550. Her first call to the station was prompted by Hillary Clinton's lament that "she could have stayed at home and baked cookies." Martha now does a daily talk radio show on WDUN in Gainesville from 9:00-11:30 am (www.wdun.com or www.marthazoller.com) and on Rightalk Radio at www.rightalk.com.

In 2005, Martha was named to the "Heavy Hundred" Talk Show Hosts in America by *Talkers Magazine.* She is a regular panelist on Fox 5 Atlanta's *The Georgia Gang,* has been seen on Fox News Channel, CNN, and MSNBC, and is a contributor to Accessnorthga.com, *Jewish World Review,* UPI, and various other publications. Martha is also available as a motivational speaker for church, community, and national groups.

In 2005, Martha added defense expert to her repertoire of talents by completing the Department of Defense's oldest civilian training program, Joint Civilian Orientation Conference. In April, Martha visited with members of all the branches of the service, saw what they can do on their bases around the country and was briefed by Secretary of Defense Donald Rumsfeld and Chairman of the Joint Chiefs of Staff General Richard Myers. In July, Martha was part of one of the first trips by radio talk show hosts to Kuwait and Iraq which included live broadcasts from Iraq. The group was briefed by General John Custer of the United States Army and General Abdul Qader Jassim of the Iraqi Army, and conducted interviews with scores of men and women in uniform.

Martha Zoller lives with her husband and children in Gainesville, Georgia.